Welcome Home

Welcome Home

A Memoir with Selected Photographs and Letters

Lucia Berlin

Edited and with a Foreword by Jeff Berlin

Farrar, Straus and Giroux   New York

Farrar, Straus and Giroux
175 Varick Street, New York 10014

Most of the chapters from the first section of *Welcome Home* have previously appeared, in slightly different form, in the journal *Square One*, no. 1 (Spring 2003) and no. 3 (Spring 2005). The last five chapters were published on newyorker.com as "Memories of Mexico" in 2016.

Library of Congress Cataloging-in-Publication Data
Names: Berlin, Lucia, author.
Title: Welcome home : a memoir with selected photographs and letters / Lucia Berlin.
Description: First edition. | New York : Farrar, Straus and Giroux, 2018.
Identifiers: LCCN 2018017727 | ISBN 9780374287597 (hardcover)
Subjects: LCSH: Berlin, Lucia. | Women authors, American—Biography. | LCGFT: Autobiographies.
Classification: LCC PS3552.E72485 Z46 2018 | DDC 813/.54 [B] —dc23
LC record available at https://lccn.loc.gov/2018017727

Designed by Jonathan D. Lippincott

Our books may be purchased in bulk for promotional, educational, or business use. Please contact your local bookseller or the Macmillan Corporate and Premium Sales Department at 1-800-221-7945, extension 5442, or by e-mail at MacmillanSpecialMarkets@macmillan.com.

www.fsgbooks.com
www.twitter.com/fsgbooks • www.facebook.com/fsgbooks

1 3 5 7 9 10 8 6 4 2

In memory of Fred Buck and Helene Dorn

Foreword

"I've lived so many places it's ridiculous . . . and because I moved so much, place is very, very important to me. I'm always looking . . . looking for home."

—Lucia Berlin, interview (2003)

The first writer I ever watched at work was my mother, Lucia Berlin. My earliest memories are of my brother Mark and me riding our tricycles around our Greenwich Village loft while Mom pounded away on her Olympia typewriter. We thought she was writing letters—she wrote a *lot* of letters. On our long walks around the city, we would stop at a mailbox almost every day, where she would let us drop her envelopes through the slot. We loved to see them disappear and hear them fall. Whenever she received a letter, she would read it to us, often making a story out of whatever had been delivered that day.

We grew up listening to her stories. We heard a lot of them, and sometimes they were our bedtime stories: her adventures with her best friend, Kentshereve; the bear that kept them captive when they were camping; the cabin with the magazine-page wallpaper; Aunt Tiny up on the roof; Uncle John's pet mountain lion—we heard them all more than once. They were stories from her life and many would find their way into the stories that she later wrote and published.

When I was around six, while exploring a closet, I discovered a typewriter case. Inside was a folder with "A Peaceable Kingdom" written on the front. It was a story about two little girls selling musical vanity boxes all around El Paso. It was the first thing I ever read that wasn't a children's book. It was then that I realized my mom wasn't just typing letters, she was writing stories. She explained to me how, a few years before, she had been published in magazines. She showed me copies of them and let me read them. After that, I often pestered her to let me read what she was working on, to which she would say, "When I'm finished."

It would be another seven or eight years before she started finishing things enough to let me read them. By this time, she had two more sons (my brothers, David and Dan), was divorced from her third husband (our Dad, Buddy Berlin), had moved to Berkeley, and was struggling to make ends meet as a teacher at a small private high school. Amid the chaos (or because of it), she wrote more than ever. Most nights, after dinner and our favorite TV show, she would park herself at the kitchen table with a glass of bourbon and start writing, often continuing late into the night. She usually scribbled longhand with a ballpoint pen into spiral notebooks, though occasionally we would be awakened by the sound of her typewriter, often drowned out by her favorite song of the moment being played over and over on the stereo.

The first stories she finished around this time were ones she had started in New York and Albuquerque in the early sixties. These soon gave way to more personal stories born out of bad situations and personal tragedies, resulting from her worsening problem with alcohol. After losing her teaching job, she took on a series of different jobs (cleaning woman, telephone operator, hospital ward clerk) that would provide rich source material for new stories, as would time spent in drunk tanks and detox wards. Despite any setbacks, she continued to write and soon began to get published again.

Years later, the last thing she had me read was an early draft of *Welcome Home*, a series of remembrances of the places she had called home. She had originally intended it to be simple sketches of the places themselves, with no characters or dialogue. These were the stories from her childhood that we had heard when we were kids but now in sequence and no longer masquerading as fiction. Unfortunately, time ran out and the last version of the manuscript ends in 1965, the last sentence unfinished.

During her life, Lucia wrote hundreds, if not thousands, of letters. Included here are some of our favorites from the same time frame as *Welcome Home*. Most of them are letters written to her good friends Ed Dorn and Helene Dorn between 1959 and 1965. It was a time of drama, growth, and upheaval, and the letters offer a fascinating look into the mind of a young mother and aspiring writer in the throes of self-discovery.

We give you *Welcome Home*; stories, letters, and photographs from the first twenty-nine years in the life of a unique American voice.

—*Jeff Berlin, May 2018*

Welcome Home

Alaska, 1935

Juneau, Alaska, 1935

Ted and Mary Brown,
Juneau, 1935

The Browns' house
in Juneau

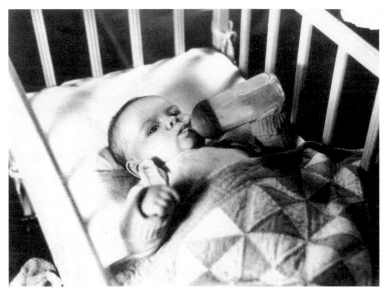

Lucia, born November 12, 1936

Juneau, Alaska

They said it was a sweet small house with many windows and sturdy woodstoves, screens taut against mosquitoes. It looked out on the bay, onto sunsets and stars and dazzling Northern Lights. My mother would rock me as she gazed down at the harbor, which was always crowded with fishing boats and tugs,

Mary Brown and Lucia, Juneau, 1937

Ted and Mary Brown, Mullan, Idaho, 1937

American and Russian ore ships. My crib was in the bedroom, where it was either very dark or very bright all the time, she told me, without further explaining the long and short lengths of the seasons. The first word I spoke was *light*.

Mullan, Idaho

My earliest memory is of pine branches brushing against a windowpane. This house was in Coeur d'Alene, Idaho, at the Sunshine Mine. Massive oak trees had branches almost parallel to the ground and squirrels raced back and forth on them as if on highways.

I recently read that the scent of flowers, especially roses and lilacs, actually was much more intense years ago, their perfume now diluted by hybridization. True or not, my remembered Idaho perfumes are more vivid than any flower today. The apple blossoms and hyacinths were literally intoxicating. I'd lie on the grass beneath the lilac tree and breathe until I became giddy. In those days I also would spin around and around until I was so dizzy I couldn't stand up. Maybe these were early warning signs and lilacs my first addiction.

The Browns' house in Mullan, 1937

Lucia, Mullan

I had never heard about pussy willows, so I was astonished to see fur growing on a stalk. I waded the icy stream to reach them, soaking my shoes and clothes. I wasn't allowed to go outside after that; I might have drowned or been swept away.

I slept on a Murphy bed. These were common then, beds that closed up inside a closet during the day. There were no rugs and very little furniture in this big house. Creaks. Echoes of wind in the trees, the splatter of rain against glass. Sobs in the bathroom.

At night sometimes my parents played pinochle with neighbors. Laughter and smoke floated up the stairs to my room. Finnish and Swedish exclamations. Lovely, the cascade of poker chips and maraca ice cubes. The particular way my mother dealt. Quick hiss of a shuffle, a crisp slap slap slap as she laid down the cards.

I watched the children go to school every morning and later I could hear them playing kickball and jacks, spinning tops. I played inside with Skippy, my "dog," a small coffee percolator tied to a bathrobe belt. My mother read mysteries. We both looked out of windows and watched it rain. At first it is scary, then beautiful, when you wake up to the day of the first snow.

My father came home from work tired and thick with grime, his eyes startled rings of white with emerald green inside.

On Saturday evenings we walked down the hill to town. A general store and post office, jail and barbershop, a drugstore and three bars. We got a *Saturday Evening Post* and a giant-size Hershey bar. Sensible crunch of snow beneath our galoshes. We started home after dark, but it was as bright as day, with Idaho stars shattering the sky. The light of stars was definitely brighter then, too.

Marion, Kentucky

Snow and cold that quickly turned into a sultry southern spring with catalpa, peach, and apple blossoms. Birds everywhere, irrepressibly jubilant. Butterflies. I had to stay on the boardinghouse veranda, which was painted glossy black and mopped by glossy nigras. "Don't let her call them that," my father said to my mother.

"I'm from Texas. Should I say darkies?"

"Colored, for God's sake."

The colored maids and cooks and waiters all talked to me.

There were no other children at the boardinghouse. The miners in Marion were single men, Mexicans, mostly, hundreds of them living in barracks. The people in the boardinghouse were engineers like my father, assayers, geologists, a bricklayer with a mustache who laughed with my mother on the veranda. The only other woman guest was a health nurse. Her breasts were so enormous she had to eat sitting sideways. I couldn't stop looking at them until my father spanked me for staring at her bosom. Then just the word *bosom* gave me the giggles but I couldn't stop saying it, singing, "Bosom bosom bosom." The nurse traveled to different schools, treating impetigo and ringworm with Gentian Violet.

We lived in one hot room with a ceiling fan and a mosquito net, a balcony big enough only for me. All the guests used a

LEFT: Lucia, Marion, Kentucky, 1939

BELOW: The boardinghouse, Marion, 1939

mildewed and foul-smelling bathroom down the hall. Sometimes I came into our room and my mother was crying, but she said, "No, I'm not, you hear?" She read mysteries lying on the bed in a peach-colored slip.

We only went out from the boardinghouse three times. Once the bricklayer took us for a drive into the country. Rolling green hills with cows and horses and then a farm with pigs. Enormous pigs as big as cars with mean little human eyes. My father drove us across the Mississippi River. He cried, looking across the expanse of it, and said we were blessed to live in America. My mother called him a sentimental sap. He took us to a big city where we rode on an escalator. I got jacks to play with on the veranda but couldn't learn how. I tried to rename Skippy Gentian Violet but it didn't take. Fireflies. Fireflies. Fireflies.

Deer Lodge, Montana

In Deer Lodge we lived in a one-bedroom log cabin at the Lonesome Pine Motor Court. Cozy, with a western motif. Brands on the lampshades. Curtains and bedspreads with cowboys and Indians on them. Paintings of broncobusters and Indian braves. Hiawatha in a canoe. I slept on the pullout couch next to a wonderful radio. During Bible shows I'd shout back at the little speaker, "Yes, Jesus is my blessed redeemer!" *The Shadow, Fibber McGee, Jack Benny, Let's Pretend.* I got the giggles whenever I heard the song "I Ain't Got Nobody," because my mother called my vagina my body, said never to play with it.

In Deer Lodge my mother had a friend, Georgia, whose husband, Joe, worked the same shift at the mine with my father. They lived next door, came over every Sunday for coffee and coffee cake my mother baked. She didn't usually cook, so she was really proud of this cake. It was always snowing outside; blazing heat came from the kitchen oven. The house was steamy, fragrant with cinnamon and vanilla. Everyone had pink shiny faces and laughed.

During the week the men were so tired they could barely get their boots off. They ate without talking and fell into bed. On Saturdays they'd all drink bourbon and play bridge and laugh. On Sundays my father and Joe took turns reading the funnies at breakfast, then lay on my bed and read the rest of the paper while the women washed up and did hairdos, rolling pompadours over hair-rats, making waves with clamps. They plucked their eyebrows and manicured their nails while the men listened to football games on the radio. I'd lie between them on the bed-couch, coloring, loving the cheers of the crowds, the frantic announcers, the men's hollering or socking each other's shoulders, their miner's smell of Camel cigarettes

Lucia, November 1940

and beer and soap. Miners always smell like soap, surely because they get so dirty.

Helena, Montana

In Helena we lived in a loud apartment where my parents slept on the Murphy bed and I on a canvas cot. Outside the back door the cream popped up from the milk bottles every morning. There was an ice storm and the trees sounded like shattering glass. I learned to read. All I really remember of Helena is the library, the green cover of *Old Mother West Wind*, the worn blue *Understood Betsy*. I believed that *Understood Betsy* had been written especially for me, that somewhere there was a person who wanted to tell me about her.

For weeks before the first snow my father took me up into the mountains every Saturday. We carried winter supplies to an old prospector who had lived alone up there some fifty

Lucia, Blue, and old Mr. Johnson at his cabin, 1941

Camping and trout fishing above Helena

years. Flour and coffee, tobacco, sugar, dried beans, salt pork, oatmeal, candles. Heavy stacks of magazines: *The Saturday Evening Post, Redbook, Field and Stream.*

It was a long hike up a trail we had blazed the first day. He let me slash the bark; the sap is still pungent in my memory. Tucked into the edge of the lush intensely green meadow was Johnson's cabin. It was an unpainted hut, really, with windows that looked like eyes and a door that was a goofy crooked smile. Tall grass and wildflowers covered the roof like a festive hat. I would lie on the roof under the blue sky, nudged and licked by dogs and goats. My father and the old man sat below me on nail kegs, drinking coffee, looking over gold nuggets he had panned, looking at all kinds of rocks, hmming and exclaiming over them. My father listened for hours to the old man's stories. Now I wish I had listened but then I just wanted to lie on the roof in a silence broken only by Steller's jays and the playful goats and dogs.

Before we left, my father went into the woods to drag back logs and branches, chopped them into stacks near the door. I carefully tore out pages from magazines and glued them onto the walls with flour and water paste, careful so as not to wet any of the text. The idea was to have a tight patchwork of pages all over the cabin, from floor to ceiling. All through the dark days of winter Johnson would read the walls. It was important to mix up the pages and magazines, so that page 20 might be high on a north wall and 21 on the bottom of the south wall.

I believe this was my first lesson in literature, in the infinite possibilities of creativity. What I knew for sure was that his walls were a great idea. He would have read through the magazines very quickly if the pages were consecutive. This way, since they were not in any order (and usually the previous or following page was pasted to the wall), whenever he read a page he had to invent the story that went with it, amending it sometimes when, days later, he would find a connected page on another wall. When he had exhausted the potentials of his cabin he would repaper it with more pages in a similarly random order.

His goats and dogs lived inside with him once the snow began. I liked to imagine them all curled up on the old brass

Lucia with Blue

Mullan, 1940

bed, watching him in his long johns as he read his walls by candlelight. He said when he got cold in bed he'd just pull up another goat.

There was an outhouse a short distance from the cabin, although he said he usually just pissed off the porch. There was also a toilet seat, centered like a throne on top of a hill. "That's for thinking," he said. "Go on up, we won't look. You can see half of Montana from up there." It seemed as if I could see it all.

Mullan, Idaho

This time we lived in one of the tarpaper cabins just above the mine. Churning and clackety-clack of engines and generators, pulleys screeching, whirring. Chains clanked. Welding rods sizzled. Scrapings and hisses and thuds. Rocks crashed and rumbled from shovels into trucks, onto conveyors. Trams creaked and rattled, whistles keened, groaned, piped. Different whistles all day and night. Men cursed and hollered day and night too, especially at night when saws would whine and all the screeching sounds turned into monsters. On the morning of the first snow, it was miraculous to see the chains and riggings, the gears and chutes transformed into glistening intricate lacework. The snow made the mine seem delicate and almost quiet. Young Mexican miners played in it like children.

There were barracks full of miners, single men, Mexicans and Finns and Basques. Most of them didn't speak English and were far from their countries and families, my father said, trying to explain why they drank and fought so much.

There was a baby now, my sister, Molly. Her crib was in my parents' room. I slept on a Murphy bed in the main room, which stayed down and was a couch during the day. I missed the radio. Now it was in the bedroom, where the baby was supposed to be asleep.

The only heat came from a potbellied stove. In the morning when it was just light enough to see my breath steam I waited for the clank of the stove door handle. In a few minutes would come the snap and crack of the wood starting to burn, the tumble of

Lucia, Mullan, 1941

Molly Keith Brown,
born October 6, 1941

a shovelful of coal. Cheerful sound of the percolator, the flick of a match on my mother's thumbnail, chunk of my father's Zippo. They let me give the baby her bottle while they had coffee. She was cozy in bed with me. She wasn't interesting, but she liked my songs. "If your head scratches, don't itch it, Fitch it. Use your head, save your hair. Use Fitch shampoo." And "I ain't got no body, ain't got nobody to carry me home."

The walls weren't painted, just wood, like the floors. I loved living in a wooden house, putting wood in the fire to keep us warm, looking out at the woods. The whole house smelled like wood.

The crisp fragrance of pine hit you when you opened the door. Once you were in the actual woods, you didn't hear the mine anymore. Everything grew quiet, even my steps on the silken needles. I would think I heard the breezes in the trees but when I stopped to listen there would be no sound.

The kitchen floor really sloped. I spent hours rolling tin cans down to the bottom. Tuna beats pineapple.

Just over our hill was a valley and another hillside where all the trees had burned down the year before. When I first saw it, the entire expanse was blanketed with scarlet Indian paintbrush. A vast blaze of red, alive and vibrating with the hum of bees.

I made a friend. Kentshereve. His house next door was just like ours except there were six children. They were very poor and the father would get bags and bags of old bread at a bakery in Wallace. For breakfast they ate soppings, bread soaked in gravy made of bacon drippings and PET milk. Once it was freezing cold and they had no coal or wood. The father kept filling the little stove with bags and bags of stale bread until finally everybody was warm, gathered around. The Lord's Prayer takes me to that kitchen.

My sister, Molly, got pneumonia and spent two days in the hospital in Wallace. I stayed next door where the children slept

Sunshine Mine, Idaho   Lucia and friends in Mullan

on hay in a loft. There was oilcloth nailed up instead of a window. Kentshereve and I took turns putting one eye to a hole in the cloth to look at the night sky. The hole seemed to act like a telescope, framing and magnifying the blinding array of stars.

I was happy lying between the children on the hay bed, happy to smell them even though they were bad smells, I suppose, urine and sour milk, dirty feet and hair. We nestled together, nuzzling like puppies as we fell asleep, all of us sucking our thumbs.

Kentshereve and I started first grade. It was far to school . . . up a high hill and then far down, up another hill and into town. After school we got rides home from Murphy's bar, where all our fathers went after their shift. The miners always toasted the first drink: "Shall we work? Hell, no! Shall we strike? Hell, no! What shall we do? Drink! Hooray!"

We loved going to school. There was only one teacher, Miss Brick, who was a fine teacher. We were each in different groups for different subjects. I was with the little kids for numbers and writing, with the big kids for reading and geography. Kentshereve was just the opposite. He was the smartest in the whole school. He knew all kinds of things, like when you chop open a tulip bulb there is a miniature tulip inside it.

Soon after Pearl Harbor my father went overseas. He had been in Navy ROTC, so he went to officer's training to become a lieutenant, then to the Pacific on an ammunition ship. We went to Granpa and Mamie's in El Paso, Texas.

This all happened very fast, a few days before the Christmas pageant, where Kentshereve and I would have been magi. (His name was Kent Shreve, but I didn't realize this for many years.) For the next long horrible years, I yearned for him and my father.

They call it heartache because missing someone is an actual physical pain, in your blood and bones.

My father took us to the Davenport Hotel in Spokane and

Lieutenant Ted Brown, U.S. Navy

then he drove away. We spent the night and took the train to Texas the next day. My mother and I each had a bed with ironed sheets. My sister slept on pillows in a drawer from a chest in the room.

My mother took the drawer to the train, with my sister in it. I was scared and shocked because she had stolen the drawer. She said, "Would you shut up about it?" and slapped me, and everything went wrong after that.

Southern Pacific Railroad, Spokane–El Paso

Except for a bunk aboard a ship in mid-ocean (in a calm sea) there is no finer place to sleep than in a Pullman car berth, rocking gently along an American plain.

There is an elegant little lamp above your head, that you can turn on or off without getting out of the rough warm covers. Beneath the windows stretches a long net bag where you can put your things away but still see where everything is. I kept my barrettes, shoes, crayons, Skippy, and an Old Maid deck in it.

The window shades slid up and down effortlessly. I lay in the dark and looked out on clouds passing over the moon, a farmhouse with one person awake in the kitchen. I turned on the light with the curtain open, then waved and smiled in case there was anybody out there in the woods. The porter came and whispered, "Is everything all right, miss?" It was nice, safe and buttoned up, knowing he was watching out for me. And the conductor was, too. When we stopped in little towns, I opened the shade a little. Once I saw the legs of two men in boots and overalls, a lantern swinging between them. They spoke easily, laughing, and then the ironed blue-black pants and shiny black shoes of the conductor met them, and all of them talked and laughed in a good way—not laughing at a joke or a person, but as if things about the world were funny.

Colts running in pastures, a little town waking up. A woman in a farmyard hanging sheets on the line. She opened a clothespin with her teeth and waved at the train.

The Pullman bed folds up even tidier than a Murphy bed and it has two beds inside, an upper and lower berth. The upper berth is good when you want to really be in a train and concentrate on all its noises or when you want to feel alone. You will sleep more since you won't be looking out the window.

Terrifying, the wind and loud space between the cars.

The doors were heavy and hard to open, but it was fun to go through all the cars and drink cold water from the white cone cups. The club car was full of servicemen and smoke, the wrong laughter.

The dining car was the finest place I had ever been. The elegance of its sparking-shocking carpet, high-backed chairs, the linen cloths and napkins. The pewter plates had lids on them; they and the silverware and pitchers were heavy and important. Sugar in cubes, served with tongs. Finger bowls with a slice of lemon in warm water. Everything about the dining room was solid and gracious, especially the waiters who were tall and gray-haired, dressed in black with long white aprons. They were soft-spoken and kind to me, to everyone. In a kitchen about two by three feet wide all the food was cooked by two really old men who talked and laughed the whole time they worked.

The best part about the bathroom on a train was that the toilet opened onto the grass and the railroad ties beneath it. I still don't know, and am embarrassed, at my advanced age, to ask if airplane toilets are the same. Is all that personal waste matter dissipating into the atmosphere? And if so, isn't there a lot of it? If not, where do they store it? I liked gazing at the ground flying past beneath the train toilet. A few times my mother threw up and I held her head, counting ties. She spent most of the trip reading in the bathroom, where there was a

Mary Brown and Lucia,
El Paso, Texas

couch and chairs. She smoked, fed my sister, and drank whiskey with another woman until they had a scary argument. The conductor made the woman get off the train in Utah. Later that night, the porter came into the bathroom. I was holding Molly; my mother was asleep. He said that my berth was made up: "Go on to bed, don't you worry none."

El Paso, Texas

When we got off the train, it seemed as if something had happened to El Paso. Surely there were trees but I didn't see any, just sun-bleached sky stretched way out in every direction above and all around. The air was heavy, slurred with heat and smelter fumes, caliche dust.

Mamie and Granpa lived on Upson Avenue, close to the smelter, so day and night the skies would suddenly grow dark with smoke. Dark cascading waves, eye-stinging and nauseatingly strong with sulfur and other metallic fumes. Lovely, though, because the sun glinted into the smoke, highlighting a billowing, iridescent kaleidoscope of colors—acid green, fuchsia, Prussian blue.

Like all the houses on that side of the street, theirs was built upon a hill, so there was a high staircase to a yellow yard, a Spitz dog named Linda tied to a spindly chinaberry tree. A wall of fragrant pink oleander bushes blocked the house next door. I went over to smell them, but Mamie said to take care now, they'd kill me ifen I etem.

Inside, it was surprisingly cool. The house was dark, the windows tightly closed to keep out the heat and the smelter dust. Dunes of dust were on the furniture and the floors.

The house smelled of sulfur, wet dirty laundry, cigarettes, whiskey, Flit, food gone bad. There wasn't a refrigerator but an icebox that always had something rotten in it. The pantry had good smells of vanilla and cloves but also potatoes or onions that were rotten, and dead mice.

El Paso, 1943

My grandmother was a poor housekeeper because they always used to have servants, my mother said. My mother didn't clean Upson either. My father had cooked and cleaned most of the time. In Texas we always had a pot roast on Sundays.

The rest of the meals varied from pork chops to peanut butter sandwiches or tomato soup unless Uncle John was home, and then we had rice and beans and tortillas, enchiladas with an egg on top, tacos, or menudo.

Everyone was always spraying Flit at cockroaches or mosquitoes. When you turned on a light at night you surprised thousands of cockroaches that clattered away. The bathroom reeked. The linoleum was all worn away, and when Granpa peed, he mostly peed on the floor. He bathed every day though, and wore starched white shirts and fine suits with vests even in summer. He smelled of Camels and bay rum and Jack Daniel's. My mother smelled of Camels and Tabu and Jack Daniel's. Uncle John smelled of Delicado cigarettes and tequila.

Mamie had many smells, all of them suffocating, as I fell

Lucia and Molly, El Paso, 1944

into her in the middle of the big bed in the center bedroom. Her skin itself was white and moist, the exact texture and temperature of Ethiopian bread.

She rubbed her poor feet with Absorbine Jr. every night and put strong-smelling medicine on her corns. Granpa was a dentist and she worked as his assistant, standing for long hours in her tight corsets. At night I'd powder her back with talcum and help her take all the pins out of her hair. I loved to brush her hair. Still black, thick and soft, it reached to the back of her knees. When she was in her nightgown she would braid her hair into one long braid. As she knelt to say her prayers she looked like a young girl.

There were oriental carpets in the living room and dining room. Both rooms were crowded with furniture, like a store. They were precious antiques, kept after they lost their home on Rim Road. Granpa's money went during the Depression; his drinking had hurt his dental practice. Although she never swept, Mamie polished her mahogany and marble-topped tables and dusted carved sideboards, polished silver for hours at a time.

There were two huge leather rocking chairs for Granpa— one by the potbellied stove in the dining room, one by the big radio in the living room. Sometimes he would catch me and make me rock in his lap even if I cried. After work he would rock and smoke, listen to H. V. Kaltenborn, and read the paper, which he burned page by page in a big red ashtray. Sometimes he would listen to the radio in the evenings. Mamie would too, with my sister beside her and her Bible in her lap. Most evenings he was at the Elks club and my mother was at the Pomeroys' playing bridge or in Juárez. The two of them ate in their own bedrooms and never spoke a word to each other. Mamie and my sister ate in the kitchen. I ate at the Duncan Phyfe table in the dining room, reading *Emily Post* and *Bartlett's Quotations*.

Uncle John would come home from Mexico or other Texan towns. He said he was wrangling cattle, which may or may not have been true. He'd repair antiques in a shop set up in the shed, working in the backyard. He slept in a sort of bedroll of old quilts on the back porch. Every day the first thing I did was check and see if he was still there, or back yet.

Everything was all right when he was at home. He made each of us laugh, and he was the only one we all talked to, who listened to each of us. He took me to cabooses and Juárez and the zoo. At night I was afraid to go down the dark hall to the bathroom, afraid of unseen ghosts and of Granpa and my mother, who would often burst from their doors like deranged cuckoos. John told me to pray, "God will take care of me. God will take care of me," and then run like hell. He'd come home drunk too at night, but sweet, teary drunk. He woke me, made me puffed wheat with vanilla and sugar. He'd ask me things and tell me things. I talked to him about Kentshereve and my father. He told me about how Dolores broke his heart. Uncle

Uncle John and his dog, Linda

John could really cook. If either of us was sad or afraid, he'd say, "This situation calls for enchiladas."

Patagonia, Arizona

The Trench Mine was an hour drive into the mountains above Patagonia. My father became the superintendent there soon after the war was over.

Is it possible that we were all happy every day that we lived there? Each one of us always remembered it so, especially my mother. She didn't drink there, wore pretty clothes. She made things to eat from *The Joy of Cooking*, even devil's food cake.

The mill superintendent, geologists, another engineer, and their wives lived in other houses on the hill. One other couple had children, one of them Billy, who was as close to Molly as Kentshereve had been to me. The two roamed all over the hill, each carrying a docile cat and pulling a wagon to carry things they found.

Trench Mine, Patagonia, Arizona

Lucia, Patagonia, 1947

The couples on the hill became good friends, played bridge and poker and canasta, had picnics and potlucks.

It was my parents' first real house. They painted the living room apple green and Molly's and my bedroom peaches and cream. They bought furniture in Nogales and found a cowboy painting in Tucson for over the couch. My father mowed the grass, grew vegetables and roses, tulips and hyacinths in the spring.

Molly and I went to the one-room schoolhouse in Harshaw. The window by my desk looked out onto the Farrells'. They bred palominos and had an apple orchard. I fell in love with Ramona, a palomino filly, watched her canter through showers of blossoms. She kicked up her heels. Interesting how often people use that strange expression. Have they all seen colts playing in a field?

After dinner, at the Trench, we'd take out the garbage. Out

to the edge of the rocky red cliff behind our house. All the food went on the compost. Cans and bottles I got to toss over the ledge. Cardboard paper we burned in a rusty old incinerator. This was the most pleasurable ritual, maybe the only one we ever had as a family. The Arizona sky was always beautiful, clear with voluptuous cumulus clouds, orange and red, as the sun set against the crags. We could see far around us and down across the valley to the jagged purple face of Mount Baldy. Sparks from the fire lit up our faces while we stood there in the growing darkness. Mabel the dog and Molly's cat, Ben, curled up in the grass, nighthawks circled above us as the evening star appeared, bats streaked past. We always watched for the very moment when the evening star came out or grew bright but it simply happened.

Deer came close to us often at the mine. Porcupines and coatis on their way down to the stream below us. Each of us saw mountain lions several times, their graceful power streaking with a whisper through manzanita bushes.

Ted gardening

Molly and Lucia, Patagonia

Hernando de Aguirre 1419, Santiago, Chile, S.A.

A two-story Tudor house on a large corner lot. It had lawns, a garden—especially fine in spring, with rhododendrons and azaleas, wisteria and iris. Fragrant fruit trees and daffodils were followed by sweet peas, stock, delphiniums, lilies, and roses all summer long until autumn's dahlias and chrysanthemums arrived. Mañuel took care of the garden, his little boy snipped off dead blossoms all day long.

We lived near Las Lilas Avenue and the starkly modern El Bosque church. This was a beautiful part of Santiago then, near Santiago College, where Molly and I went to school.

The house was small and elegant, with French doors opening to the garden. It had parquet floors and a marble fireplace. Our bedroom window opened to the clear blue sky and the snow-covered Andes, looked down onto the tree-lined avenue. Our room always smelled like hyacinth, although this must have only been for a few weeks.

The Andes seemed to have no foothills. Aconcagua shot straight up, incredibly high, into jagged regal peaks, the snow changing colors all day, flaming each evening into magenta, red, coral, or soft yellow.

The furniture was garish "antique" French. My mother wept when it arrived. "Oh, I knew it was all wrong." The paintings were all wrong too, but in a nice way, sort of out-of-focus Corot. There were many gigantic gilt-framed mirrors because she was so nervous about choosing paintings. Chandeliers blazed in the living and dining rooms, terrifying with their crazed tinkling during the frequent earthquakes.

Maria and Rosa slept in a tiny room off the kitchen. My father told them what to do at first, but as I learned Spanish quickly it ended up that I took over the household, gave them orders, chose the menus, gave them money for shopping, checked the receipts, scolded them.

On the way to Santiago, 1949

I couldn't get Maria and Rosa to use the washing machine in the garage so I did the washing and they hung the clothes to dry. There was no Kotex in those days so like all the other maids they would spend hours sitting on the lawn with a tub and a hose, washing bloody rags.

There was a bell on the floor under the immense dining room table. I ate there alone; I loved to ring for each course. My father dined out, or was traveling to mines in Bolivia or Peru or northern Chile. Molly had dinner early with Maria and Rosa in the kitchen, and Mama always ate in bed.

She stayed mostly in bed now. She was intimidated by the Santiago social scene, was comfortable only playing bridge with an English couple called the Mortimers or poker with a group of Jesuit priests.

At the back of the downstairs was a large room that opened onto a flagstone terrace. We called it the family room but I was the only one who used it, for *bailoteos* every week with my friends from school, Chilean and English girls, and boys from the Grange, an elite Eton-type academy. We danced to tangos and rumbas. "Night and Day," "Frenesi," "Adios Muchachos," Charles Trenet's "La Mer," "My Foolish Heart." We never danced cheek to cheek, never held hands, and surely never kissed unless we were *pololeando*, or going steady.

I was very pretty, wore beautiful clothes, and all of my friends were as frivolous and pampered as I was. We went to dressmakers and hairdressers and cobblers, out to lunch at the Carrera or the Ahumada, to lavish teas at the Crillon or at each other's houses.

We skied in Portillo all winter, spent summers in Algarrobo and Viña del Mar. We watched rugby and cricket matches, played tennis and golf, swam at the Prince of Wales Country Club. On weekends there were movies and nightclubs and balls; we often ended up at El Bosque's early Mass in evening clothes. When Molly and I woke up every morning we rang for our breakfast. One push was for *café con leche*, two for cocoa,

Molly and Lucia, 1952

32

with our fruit and toast. At night Rosa put hot bricks inside the sheets, at the foot of each bed, and laid out our school uniforms for the next day. Dark green wool with crisp starched white collars and cuffs, brown stockings and sturdy shoes, brown blazer and round brimmed hat with a ribbon. A clean starched white apron, more like a lab coat, that we wore over our uniforms at school. We carried book bags on the long walk to school along the tree-lined streets, past beautiful houses and gardens. This was many years before the revolution; opulence and ease enveloped our world then.

Santiago College was a fine old stone building with three large wings under red-tiled roofs. It had wisteria-covered arches, shining tile floors on the verandas, was built around a vast rose garden with benches, raked paths. On a lower level was a theater and a gymnasium, a field for hockey and badminton. There were many elm and maple trees, fruit trees, another large garden with a fountain outside the Upper School.

Classes were hard; all but English were taught in Spanish. Except for Spanish literature we had no books. The teachers

Santiago College, December 1953. Beatriz Reyes, Gail Yarborough, Lorna Gladstone, Consuelo "Conchi" Capellini, and Lucia.
(Photograph courtesy of Lorna Jury Gladstone)

would lecture without a break for an hour and we wrote down every word. For months I did this, then corrected what I had done from another girl's book, in order to write it out word for word on the tests. I did well in history and philosophy exams long before I understood what I wrote. School was very difficult. We had English and French, chemistry, math, and physics. In our Spanish class we read more Spanish and South American novels and poetry than I did later in graduate school. We read *Don Quijote* for two years, discussing the chapters in detail every day. One day in class, I read a passage where one of Cervantes's characters, in an insane asylum, says that he could make it rain whenever he felt like it. I understood in that moment that writers could do anything they wanted to do.

We had earthquake drills once a month, when we put on our hats and gloves, lined up two by two, and marched swiftly and quietly down to the rose garden. About every two or three months we had a real earthquake, never a bad one, but the

University of New
Mexico, 1954

34

teachers all remembered the bad one. Señor Peña, the physics teacher, knocked me down once as he bolted for the door. Years later a number of my classmates died during the revolution. Some were killed fighting in it, others committed suicide later because the world they knew had vanished.

Hokona Hall, University of New Mexico, Albuquerque, New Mexico

A pretty campus with big cottonwoods and elm trees, old adobe buildings. The rugged mountains and desert opened out, like Texas, with faded-denim sky all around. I had a roommate called Suzanne whose mother sent Kotex from Oklahoma every month. I didn't know the English phrase then but I wrote to my Chilean friends the equivalent of "She's not our sort." She and I agreed on green curtains and green chenille bedspreads. I put Van Gogh's sunflowers on my wall, photographs of Jutta and me in Pucón, Conchi and me on skis, the Grange rugby team.

Everything about the United States was strange to me. Most of my classes were enormous and superficial. I was allowed to take upper-division Spanish classes, with one of my favorite writers, Ramón Sender, a Spanish exile.

I majored in journalism by mistake. I wanted to be a writer, not a journalist. I loved my job as a proofreader, though. I had my own key to the dorm and was allowed to come in late.

Lou Suarez was the sportswriter. He was one of the few Mexican-American students then. He was thirty, in school on the G.I. Bill. At first I was just happy to talk in Spanish with someone kind and funny and sharp, but then we fell in love.

Most people think that their love is more wonderful than any other love has ever been. It was my first love. I thought all people felt like we did when they were in love. It was only later that I realized ours was more wonderful than any other.

Tomás and Elena, the janitor and his wife, gave us a key to the broom closet. We locked the door and climbed a ladder to the roof where we had a mattress under a canopy of cottonwoods. We made love and talked between classes, after work, all night until I crept back to the dorm before the housemother woke up. The building was surrounded by old cottonwoods. We lay beneath their branches, saw glimpses of stars and the moon. The ledge around the roof also hid us and the ice chest for beer, a lantern to read and study by. We invited Tomás and Elena to candlelit dinners, with Hamm's beer and hamburgers from the Pig Pen across Central (Route 66).

Our bower went undetected even when winter came and we had to crawl across the roof to our tarp-covered bed. We made love and talked and talked, read aloud to each other for many months.

The housemother found out somehow. She sent a telegram to my parents telling them that I was having sex with a Mexican on the roof. Stop.

They flew up on New Year's Day, stayed for two days. They decided to take me out of school after summer session to spend a year in Europe. My father offered Lou money not to see me anymore. Lou spat in my father's face. But then he and I had a horrible fight. He wanted me to marry him right then. I was seventeen, wasn't ready to yet, I said, and he pushed me out of the car.

I kept hoping that he would call me, that any day he would appear, but he never did.

Lead Street, Albuquerque

I met Paul Suttman a few months later, married him just before the SS *Stavangerfjord* was to sail for Europe. At the time I thought I was in love, didn't think I was marrying him so as not to go to Europe. I didn't feel toward Paul the trust and ten-

Albuquerque, 1956

Mr. and Mrs. Paul Suttman, 1956

derness I had for Lou. I was awed by him. He was a sculptor, a brilliant, dynamic man.

I held the hot part of the cup and gave him the handle. I ironed his jockey shorts so they would be warm. I always tell these things and everybody laughs, but, well, they are true.

I dressed as he told me to: always in black or white. My long hair was dyed black, ironed straight every morning. I wore heavy eye makeup and no lipstick. He made me sleep lying facedown on the pillow, hoping to correct my "main flaw," a turned-up nose. Of course there was the big flaw, my scoliosis. The first time he saw my naked back, he said, "Oh God—you are asymmetrical."

As we sat in restaurants or at bars, or even at our modern teak table on hard teak chairs, he would arrange my body parts. Tilt my chin up, or turn it slightly to the left, take my hands off the table, have me leaning on one elbow with one hand open, as if testing for rain, cross or uncross my legs. He said that I smiled too much and that I made too much noise during sex.

Paul chose all the furniture in the house. Black and white and earth colors. Java temple birds in a black cage had the faintest touch of pink on their throats. Mondrians on the wall, pewter Nambé ware ashtrays, Acoma and Santo Domingo pottery, a fine Navajo rug. Our dishes were black, our stainless a daring modern style. The forks had only two tines, so it was difficult to eat spaghetti.

We had our first child to keep Paul from being drafted.

Lucia with first son, Mark, born September 30, 1956

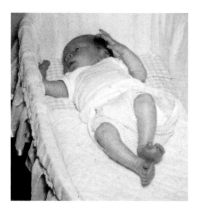

Baby Mark

Paul Suttman

I accidentally got pregnant again when Mark was only a few months old. Paul said the only solution was for him to leave, so he did. He had a grant, a patron, a villa and foundry in Florence, and a new straight-nosed girlfriend.

The morning he left, the first thing I did was to give the birds to an old lady across the street. I took down the Mondrians, put up my sunflowers and an Elvis poster, tossed a gaudy Mexican blanket over the ecru couch. I put on pink lipstick, braided my hair into pigtails.

I was smoking cigarettes borrowed from next door, my bare feet were up on the table. The dishes were unwashed. Mark crawled around in a soaking-wet diaper, pulling pans out of the cupboard. Joe Turner was singing the blues on the hi-fi when Paul came in the door. He had only been gone for about twenty minutes when his car broke down. He didn't think it was funny at all. We didn't see him again for sixteen years.

Corrales Road, Alameda, New Mexico

I met Race the night before Jeff was born. I had gone to the Skyline Club with friends to hear Prince Bobby Jack's blues and jazz band. Ernie Jones was on bass and Race Newton on piano. When we were introduced Race asked, "Do you believe in prenatal influence?"

Jeff was born the next morning and Race came with my friends to the hospital. I saw him often in the next few months. He helped a lot, playing with Mark, going to the store.

He wanted to marry me, to take care of me and my children. "I'm going to take care of you," he said.

We lived in an old adobe with thick walls, wooden vigas, and pine floors, wavery old glass in the windows. It sat in a grove of cottonwood trees, faced an apple orchard, fields of corn and alfalfa, the majestic Sandia Mountains. There were green fields all around us alive with red-winged blackbirds, thrashers, pheasants, and quail.

The house had no refrigerator and no sink or stove. There was a woodstove that worked fine but it made the kitchen really hot. The hard part with two babies in diapers was not having running water. I bathed them in a tub out by the pump,

The adobe house with a tin roof, Corrales Road, Alameda

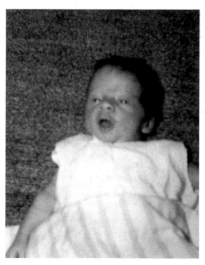

Second son, Jeff,
born April 26, 1958

boiled water for dishes on the stove. We had an outhouse that we shared with Pete, who lived in a small house next to us. Pete, well.

Race showered and changed at Ernie's house. I bathed in the metal tub on the kitchen floor, washed diapers at Bobbie's in her wringer washer, or at the laundromat on Fourth Street.

Bob and Bobbie Creeley lived down the road from us. Staying with them were Ed and Helene Dorn who had just come from Washington. Bob and Ed were poets. The three men talked about music and poetry while Bobbie, Helene, and I cooked, folded laundry, tended to the children.

We all talked and laughed for hours over Gallo wine. Other writers and musicians came through Albuquerque. Allen Ginsberg, Jack Kerouac, Gerry Mulligan, Dick Twardzik, Percy Heath. John Chamberlain, the sculptor, came, so did Stan Brakhage, a filmmaker. We all felt that we were part of an exciting era, for poetry and painting, jazz. We listened to John Coltrane and Miles Davis, tapes of readings by Charles Olson, Robert Duncan, and Lenny Bruce in performance.

Mark and Lucia

Jeff and Mark, Corrales Road, Alameda

Most of the time, though, the boys and I were alone in the white house, fending off Pete when he came home drunk but calling on him when I had no water to prime the pump. (He used Hamm's beer.) Buddy Berlin used to play saxophone with Race and Ernie Jones in the afternoons. Hot afternoons, when Race was gone, Buddy often came to take me and the boys out for root beer floats. Sometimes he brought a big thermos of frozen daiquiris. He and I would listen to Charlie Parker or Lester Young, sitting on the back stoop.

Canyon Road, Santa Fe, New Mexico

Boxy little house, surrounded by sage and lilac tamarisk. It had a kitchen with a good gas stove, a washing machine, and a fireplace. It was big enough for the Dorns and their three children as well as us.

Helene and I read Beatrix Potter to the children, baked bread, sewed and ironed while Ed and Race were at work. Race played piano, Ed was headwaiter at Claude's on Canyon Road. It was the "in" restaurant then for the Santa Fe artists and witty rich people who collected santos, Indian crafts, and jewelry.

Helene and I woke up when the men came home, their tuxedos smelling of cigarette smoke. The children would all be asleep on the living room floor near the fire while we sat at the kitchen table, drinking wine, eating still-warm just-baked bread and cheese. The two men counted their tip money and ranted about the Santa Fe art snobs, about Claude herself. She looked like Charles Laughton in drag. Velvet Navajo shirt, squash blossom necklace, squaw boots. The food at Claude's was excellent and of course the music and service were exceptional. Oh, they hated it. Imagine Ed Dorn calling anybody "sir" and Race playing "Shine On, Harvest Moon."

We read many books that winter. All of W. H. Hudson and Thomas Hardy. All my life, reading had been my private solace. I loved sharing books with Ed and Helene (Race was practicing or sleeping), reading passages out loud, talking about the characters, the places—Hudson's pampas, Hardy's Wessex.

Sometimes Buddy would drive up from Albuquerque.

Race Newton playing at Claude's in Santa Fe

Mark and Jeff
in New York

Helene would stay with the children and I'd go with Buddy to Claude's to hear Race play. Ed handed us menus, poured the cabernet, hissed at me that this was a cheap and predictable situation.

West Thirteenth Street, New York City

Race forgave me for the affair with Buddy, I think; we certainly never spoke of it. We were going to have a new life in New York. At first we lived in a laughably small studio apartment on Thirteenth Street, on the fifth floor. It was bright and sunny with windows opening out onto rooftops with vents like minarets. Pigeons and lost blue parakeets.

The first night I sat in the window, looking at a real fire escape and glimpses of pink sunset between the brick buildings. People in other apartments were screaming at each other or talking softly, sweetly. I was thrilled. This is life. This is New York! Then I realized that I was hearing people talking on television, which I hadn't known before.

I got a job with an antiques dealer on the first floor, brushing prints with tea or vinegar, dotting them with tiny flyspecks to make them look older. Aside from him, the super, and Mrs. Armitage, the old lady beneath us, the children always running running above her, I never met anybody else. Well, Freddie Greenwell.

Race couldn't join the union for a year, had to play strip joints in Yonkers, bar mitzvahs and weddings in New Jersey, Long Island. I made much of our money by sewing children's clothes, had the idea of making bright woolen ponchos for babies and toddlers, sold them in a Village shop. They were a hit, so I spent hours sewing fringe on bright woolen fabric I got in scrap bins on Seventh Avenue.

The children and I left early in the morning so Race could sleep. We went to Washington Square or to Central Park, the Natural History Museum. We rode the Staten Island Ferry often, took subways, getting off at new stops each time, learning neighborhoods. Mark pushed Jeff in his stroller, loved the Guggenheim.

It took so long to climb the stairs to the fifth floor. Many

Mark, Jeff, and Lucia
in Central Park

trips up and down, carrying Jeff and the stroller, laundry, or groceries. While they napped, Race played the piano. It seemed that he slept or played the piano or was gone. He rarely spoke to me. At night I sewed or read, wrote to Ed and Helene, talked to Symphony Sid or to Buddy when he called.

Greenwich Street, New York City

Wonderful. Race and I better now, making love again so sweet but still he rarely spoke to me. We went to many fine exhibits. Robert Frank, Richard Diebenkorn, Mark Rothko, Alberto Giacometti. We heard Miles, Bill Evans with Scott LaFaro, Coltrane, Thelonious Monk, Dizzy Gillespie, many others.

Good musicians like Wayne Shorter, Jimmy Knepper, Freddie Greenwell came to jam with Race in our loft. He was sounding great.

All of us were happier here. Race could play, I could read or write with some space between me and the boys. The boys had room to run around, ride trikes, and play without waking

**Race Newton,
Greenwich Village**

Lucia, Greenwich Village

him. Room for a double bed for us and a real round table to eat on.

The loft was above a ham-smoking factory. It had tall windows all across one end facing the Hudson. It was in a spot that later would be part of the World Trade Center site. Then it faced Washington Market, which came alive every night with blocks and blocks of produce. Brilliant oranges, limes, apples, all sorts of fruits and vegetables were sold until six in the morning. Just across the street from us, and for many blocks around, were parking lots which were empty at night and all weekend. Mark and Jeff rode their trikes, played with their wagon or balls, sleds when it snowed.

Their room had been a machine shop. Race turned it into a playground complete with jungle gym, a slide, two swings. He also made them a fine wooden toy box, painted shiny red. God, what a good man he was, silently kind. His silence felt like a cruelty to me.

The previous tenants were painters and had left many of their enormous canvases, mostly swathes of colors, which we used to make walls, changing the place around like a dollhouse.

Jeff, winter 1960

Mark in Washington
Square Park

The roof was our yard, with clothesline and garden, chairs
to look out and watch the tugboats and barges, the elegant lin-
ers going out to sea, to look over at City Hall, at Trinity Church.

Denise Levertov and Mitch Goodman and their son
moved in upstairs, which was a real apartment. We all liked
our new place, explored our neighborhood. Down the street
were the Fulton Fish Market and Treflich's pet shop. Mark and
Jeff had a job there. While we drank coffee next door, they
would teach a parrot to say "Hello, Seymour!" by saying this to
him over and over, every day for about an hour, for a week or

two, until the parrot squawked "Hello, Seymour!" incessantly. It would only take a few days for some Wall Street man named Seymour to pass by, heading down to Fulton Street for lunch, and of course he would have to get the bird. Then Mark and Jeff would start on a new one.

"Whatcha know, Joe?" or "Run, Sammy, run!"

Nights were quiet. Until the produce markets opened at midnight there were few cars. I'd watch small boats and barges going downriver, men in doorways huddled close, passing a bottle, warming themselves over an oil-drum fire. Sometimes an old sailmaker drove by in a creaking horse-drawn cart.

Winter was hard. The heat and the hot water went off at five and all weekend long. The boys slept in earmuffs and mittens. I wrote by the oven, wearing gloves. We went to warm places during the day. Hottest were the Brooklyn Museum, the Hayden Planetarium, and Klein's on Fourteenth Street.

One really cold night I made a bedroom for the boys around the oven, nailing three smallish paintings together. But then I was out in the cold, which I said out loud, and I was laughing at myself when Buddy knocked on the door. He brought a bottle of brandy and four tickets to Acapulco.

Mirador Hotel, Acapulco, Mexico

My memories of Acapulco come in snapshots, like the childlike drawings in *Babar the Elephant*. Palm trees above the hotel on the edge of the cliffs. The boys in sailor suits rode rented blue tricycles around and around a track ringed with red canvas. Brightly colored taxis. Parrots in cafés with wooden fans. Buddy and I sat on wrought-iron benches in front of the church, Mark and Jeff shot marbles with a new friend on the grass in the plaza. Sandcastles on the beach, the boys brown, with red pails and shovels, arms akimbo. Buddy and I kissed

Acapulco, Mexico, 1961

Lucia, Jeff, and Mark in Acapulco

inside a blue-and-white beach cabana. All of us laughing in the calm waves at Caleta Beach.

The wooden shutters of our room let in the scent of ginger and tuberoses, moonlight and stars, the sound of the surf. In the morning, we took a funicular down to a green-tiled pool set into the rocks by the ocean. Waves crashed against the rocks, misting us with spray. I lay flat on the hot cement, eyes level with the pool, watching Buddy teach the boys to swim. Even when he was not holding them to teach them, he would hold them, or me.

We met people, on the beach, in the plaza, at cafés. People liked us, invited us over to their table, home for tea. Flamenco dancers gave us tickets to concerts; a trapeze artist asked us to the circus. Manuel, one of the divers at La Quebrada, joined us for a drink, then had us over every Sunday for steamed clams with his wife and children. We spent most evenings with Don and Maria, who became close friends for many years. Maria and I talked while Don and Buddy played chess and the boys colored and read until they fell asleep.

We went out often to dinner with Jacques and Michele, a French couple whose little girl, Marie, played with Mark and Jeff at the beach. We went to parties at Teddy Stauffer's with Acapulco society people and movie stars, to concerts with a Mexican doctor and his wife. When the boys and I were in New York, we chatted, sometimes they chattered, but now in

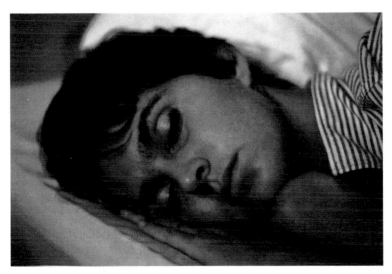

Acapulco

Acapulco the three of us were talking all the time, in English and Spanish . . . the boys even in French! Everybody embraced us hello and kissed us goodbye.

Just after we got to Mexico, I woke up one night and Buddy wasn't next to me. Sleepy, I went into the bathroom, where I found him shooting heroin. I wasn't as shocked as I would have been if I had known what heroin was, what addiction was. He said he was going to get off it, even though it would be rough for a few days.

It was bad food poisoning, we told people. Diarrhea, I told our friend the doctor, who didn't give me paregoric, prescribed tea and apple. Jacques and Michele took the boys boating and to the beach for several days; after that we went to the usually empty pool by the ocean. The boys spent hours diving over and over into the water. We all played Monopoly, ate enchiladas *suizas*, drank lemonade. Buddy shook violently under his towel in the sunshine.

He got well finally, and then weeks went by, busy and lazy, such warmhearted weeks. The heroin became but a quick scary moment. After several months, we were ready to go home to New Mexico. I would divorce Race and we would be married.

Buddy and his wife, Wuzza, had lived and traveled for years, mostly in Spain, on her money. He had studied bull-fighting, had continued to play saxophone and race Porsche Spyders. She finally insisted that he do something; so, with her backing, he got one of the first Volkswagen franchises in the west, back when the few VW drivers waved to one another on the road.

In only a few years he paid her back, had made so much money that there was no need for him ever to do anything at all.

Buddy enjoyed. He did this so well. He really enjoyed people and music, books and paintings. The next enthusiasms would be Native American culture and history, photography and flying. Oh, and the three of us.

Buddy Berlin, Acapulco

We thought then that our love would protect us from heroin, that we were starting out on a new life.

Nate Bishop came to fly us back in the new Beechcraft Bonanza, a tax write-off that Buddy was going to learn to fly.

Maybe that's where Babar came from—our toy red plane. We circled low over the city and its lovely bays, white sand, tile roofs, and palms, a crayon-blue sea. Oh, we had all been so happy there, with the old lady and the monkey.

An hour out of Albuquerque, Buddy started to shake. His nose was running and he had cramps in his legs. As soon as the plane landed, he took off to make a phone call.

Edith Boulevard, Albuquerque, New Mexico

A sprawling old adobe with fireplaces in most of the rooms. Bedrooms, baths, pantries, and studies had been added on over the years, at different levels, in every direction, but every new room had the same three-foot-wide walls, high windows facing the pool and garden. The front entrance opened into the huge wood-plank-floored kitchen, the main room of the house. In the old days this had been the hacienda, set among acres and acres of grazing land. Now it was hidden in an industrial area, with lumberyards and sheet-metal shops nearby, a car-parts dump on one side and a school-bus yard on the other side. In

Edith Boulevard, Albuquerque, New Mexico, 1962

Lucia, Edith Boulevard

back of us in a tiny house lived the Luceros, with two children in their early teens, many ducks and chickens, and a cow.

I learned fear here. My fear of the drug dealers, my fear of the drug, their fear of the narcs, one another, of not having a fix. The house, hidden away as it was, with thick walls that kept out all sound, enhanced the feeling of always hiding, sneaking. With addiction comes hiding, lying, suspicion. "You only look in my eyes now to see if they are pinned," he said. True.

Those first years on Edith went by with him on and off heroin, with us all in and out of happiness. Each time he went through a run on drugs and still another withdrawal, I swore that was the end.

He was not just a seducer or charmer. Well, yes, he was. He was sexy and charming, sharp and witty. His energy lit up any room he walked into. When the boys saw him, they didn't just say, "Hello, Dad!," but immediately ran over to touch him, hug him. So did I.

We climbed and explored Acoma and Bandelier, Mesa Verde, went to Indian dances and ceremonials and powwows. Camped out at Canyon de Chelly and Chaco. Awoke late at

Lucia, Edith Boulevard

The Berlins and the Dorns

Buddy with Jeff and Mark

night under the stars, wondering what the people living there had been like.

We had many good friends then. Bill and Martha Eastlake, the Creeleys, Liz and Jay in Taos. Buddy got his flying license. We all loved the plane. In the evening, we would fly into the sunset, red and orange cumulus all around us, on and on we

Lucia and Jeff

flew, with the colors toward the west. Buddy used to fly to Pocatello to visit the Dorns, or he would fly up and bring them
down. We flew several times to Boston to visit Buddy's family,
stopping to refuel in small towns that had no highways going
through, whose people hadn't seen tourists ever, that seemed
preserved in another era. Amish towns were the most obvious,
but other remote towns in Kansas and Tennessee seemed almost to have their own language, and were as strange to us as
we to them. We would land on crop dusters' strips—fields with
only a gas tank and a wind sock—get gas and a pickup ride to
the town café, where Buddy would get even the most suspi-
cious farmers to warm to him and talk to us.

We flew often to Puerto Vallarta, a small town then with
no road to it and no commercial flights. In summer when the
sky was billowing with clouds, the four of us would go up in
the Bonanza to watch the sun set over Albuquerque, flying low
over the flaming-red foothills, then banking around to follow
the spill and tumble of colors all the way into Arizona, back
again just in time for dusk. Every time, the boys fell asleep just
as we landed.

In the summer on Edith, we had barbecues, big parties where we ate lobster and clams we had shipped in from Maine. The pool was always full of children—the boys and their friends played until dark in the desert and junk yards around our place.

When he was on drugs, our house turned into a bunker, the doors always closed and locked. "Buddy's sick," I'd say, just like Mamie. Only Junie or Frankie, Nacho, Pete, Noodles would come. The predators who followed him to work, to the bank, who knocked at night on our door. Whispers. Raspy laughter in the dark.

David was born. Buddy had had to leave me at the hospital to go home and get a fix, so it was my second child born "with no man to hold my hand." Still, he was overjoyed with our beautiful baby, wanted now desperately to get clean. Just having needle marks would put you in jail in those days; there were no treatment programs for addicts. When David was only a few weeks old, we went to Seattle, where a doctor was allegedly curing addicts by changing their blood, adding coenzymes to the new blood. This was a nightmarish week,

Lucia, Puerto Vallarta

with blood dripping into his arm all day long in a stifling little room.

But the nights in our fine Olympia hotel room were sweet . . . the two of us with our new baby, talking all night. We would plan our move to Mexico, to Puerto Vallarta, away from the dealers. Teach the boys at home, raise them away from all the violence,

Third son, David, born September 20, 1962

Lucia and David, 1963

Lucia and boys, Albuquerque

greed, racism, and consumerism. We would lead a simple, clean, and loving life.

Yelapa, Jalisco, Mexico

Here is how I once wrote about our house in the village south of Puerto Vallarta:

> The floor of the house was fine white sand. In the mornings, our maid Pila and I raked and swept the sand, checking for scorpions, sweeping it smooth. For the first hour I would yell at the boys, "Don't walk on my floor!" as if it were waxed linoleum. Every six months, One-Eyed Luis would come in with his mule and carry out saddlebags of sand, making countless trips to the beach for fresh white sparkling sand washed up by the sea.
>
> The house was a *palapa*, the roof made of thatched palm. Three roofs, for there was a tall rectangular structure met on

each end by a semicircle. The house had the majesty of an old Victorian ferryboat; that's how it got the name *la barca de la ilusión*. Inside, cool, the ceiling was vast, supported by tall posts of ironwood, crossbars lashed together with *guacamote* vine. The house was like a cathedral, especially at night when stars or moonlight glowed through the skylights where the roofs joined. Except for an adobe room beneath the *tapanco*, there were no walls.

Buddy and I slept on a mattress in the *tapanco*, a large loft made of the veins of palm trees. When it was cold, all three boys slept in the adobe room, but usually Mark slept in a hammock in the large living room and Jeff outside next to the datura. The datura bloomed in a profusion of white flowers that hung heavy clumsily until night, when the moonlight or starlight gave the petals an opalescent shimmer of silver and the plant's intoxicating scent wafted everywhere in the house, out to the lagoon.

Most of the other flowers had no perfume and were safe from ants. Bougainvillea and hibiscus, canna lilies, four o'clocks,

The beach and lagoon in Yelapa

impatiens, zinnias. The stocks and gardenias and roses were heady with perfume, alive with butterflies of every color.

At night, my neighbor Teodora and I patrolled the gardens and the coconut grove with our lanterns, killing the swift columns of cutter ants, pouring kerosene into the nests of the ants who ate our tomatoes and green beans, lettuce and squash. Teodora had taught me to plant during the new moon and to prune when it was full, to tie jugs of water onto the lower branches of mango trees if they weren't bearing fruit.

Jeff and Mark ranged between first and fifth grades in arithmetic and spelling. Jeff loved fractions and decimals, a mystery to Mark and me. Mark read everything from children's books to *I, Claudius*. Every morning, the boys had school at the big wooden table. Scratching, sighing, giggling, they leaned their bare brown backs over marbled copybooks, Big Chief tablets.

The house was built at the edge of a coconut grove on the bank of the river. Across the river was the beach and the perfect small bay of Yelapa. Up the rocks from the beach, south over the hill, was the village, above a small cove. High mountains surrounded the bay, so there were no roads to Yelapa.

The house in Yelapa, *la barca de la ilusión*

David in the Yelapa lagoon

Horse trails through the dense jungle to Tuito, to Chacala, hours away.

The river changed all year long. Sometimes deep, swift, and green, sometimes just a stream. Sometimes, depending on the tides, the beach would close up and the river would turn into a lagoon. This was the best time, with ducks, blue heron, and egrets. The boys would spend hours playing in their dugouts, tossing nets for fish, ferrying passengers across from the beach. Even David could handle a canoe, and he was only three.

After the rains began, the water would come, at first in wild torrents. Carrying boughs of flowers, branches of oranges, dead chickens, a cow once, the swirling muddy water would break through the beach with an enormous gasp and suck of sand, swirling out into the turquoise ocean. As the days passed, the river water grew clean and sweet, and the warm rock pools filled with water for baths and washing.

Our garden grew. Buddy and the boys speared fish, caught lobster, gathered clams. We became a part of the village and

Jeff, David, and Lucia on the beach

of the bay and jungle around us; each day was full, each day was quiet.

Our mornings began with the hundreds of roosters from town, the squawks of Teodora's chickens. The boys sat at the table eating oatmeal while Buddy and I drank *café con leche* in the garden, inside the pig fence that protected the flowers. The gulls came with an enormous clapping and calling, a staccato swift flapping up the river, then a swoop back down, dispersing out to sea, calling calling, "Wake up, all is well." Every morning, when the gulls came, for the next year or so, we would look into each other's eyes, confirming the happiness and gratitude we felt, too fearful to actually say it out loud. And then we stopped that look, and for all I know, the gulls stopped coming.

First, Peggy sent a little box with a dozen vials of pure morphine. "A little something for Bud."

Peggy lived alone in a fabulous house on top of the hill. She spent much of her day looking through a powerful telescope, checking the beach for arrivals of famous people to invite up to her house, checking out everything else going on. She must have seen the boys playing soccer with village boys, riding horseback on the beach, going upriver with Juanito to help his father pick coffee. She must have seen them racing canoes, heard their laughter echoing above the water. She must have seen us talking with friends in our beautiful garden, lying on the beach. She must have seen Buddy and me kiss, must have seen us happy. How could she send that box?

And then, as if addiction had sent out loud heartbeat messages, the drug dealers began to show up. Tino or Victor, Alejandro. All young, handsome ex–beach boys, smart and mean. Whispers in our garden, laughter in the dark by the datura tree.

Southern Mexico, Volkswagen Van

Our VW van had a Porsche engine, other modifications that made it good for tough Mexican roads. Buddy and I had fixed up the back for travel. The entire back seat was a comfortable bed, with a hammock for David. The two doors opened to cupboards under the beds. Easy to get to lanterns, books, crayons, water, food, an ice chest, and a Coleman stove. Hammocks we could hang and make ourselves at home anywhere, even for a short nap while the kids played on a beach or in a forest.

We were headed for Guatemala to renew our tourist permits, we were headed away from heroin. But there was no hurry. We stayed for days in Guadalajara, spending mornings at the market, eating *birria*, strolling the aisles as if we were in a museum. Each stand was arranged with artistry and flair, whether it was squash blossoms, wreaths of garlic, intricately painted birdcages (with dozens of species of birds), pink-and-green candies, *huaraches*.

There was a Henry Moore exhibit at the museum. El Cordobés was at the bullring. Buddy considered him a shameless showoff, but the boys were thrilled by the pageantry, the

Southern Mexico

danger and grace. We stayed at a fine old hotel there, ate baby squab, *guisantes*, fine Mexican cuisine. From there we went to Ajijic. A nice pension there, but so many Americans, and such drunk ones, that we camped out for several days instead. In this way we traveled down to Guatemala. Sleeping in the woods by a river sometimes, or near some town or a small ruin that we could explore. Which meant just climbing and circling and talking about what it must have been, and each of us pretending we were there then.

We had great days camped near Teotihuacán. On the trip, I read out loud from Bernal Díaz, so the place was real to us all. Mark and Jeff both cried over Moctezuma's betrayal . . . he was a hero to them. We explored all of the temples, spent hours in the museum. We all took turns carrying or pushing David in his stroller. He was a total pain on this trip. He was used to running free, unhampered and even undiapered, going nonstop all day until he collapsed for the night. When we stopped somewhere, he ran around happily in a plaza or a café. He was so beautiful that people came over to speak with us; he made us many friends. A few times Indians made the sign of the cross on his forehead. Many women would kiss him and say *"pobrecito"*—poor thing, so lovely to have to live in this cruel world. People would borrow him, take him to the kitchen or carry him around the plaza.

Oaxaca

We traveled well. Driving made David fall asleep, thank God, and the boys colored or read or played games with Buddy and me. I would read articles or poetry to Buddy, we'd talk, laugh. It only took one of us to say, "Let's stop here!" "Okay. Let's go," Buddy would say, and we'd all get out, check it out, swim at the perfect beach, eat brain tacos at a tiny roadside stand with the sweet family, watch the white horse cantering in the field. That zest in him . . . the way he went for it, all of it. I can understand his doing drugs. I hate them for taking him from us.

Before we even saw Monte Albán or Mitla, we loved Oaxaca. The gentle faces of the Mixteca, the pastel pinks and greens of the laborers' shirts, the color of the rocks and dirt. The ancient truth of the place. We spent the night in the old colonial hotel on the plaza, ate shrimp tamales wrapped in banana leaves. We spent the evening in the plaza, listening to marimbas. Buddy and I sat on a wrought-iron bench with David while Mark and Jeff played marbles with two boys. Vendors approached us with pottery, weavings; children sold us Chiclets. Their voices and the soft conversations of couples circling the

Lucia in Oaxaca

Jeff in Oaxaca

plaza were like birdsong: Zapotecs and Mixtecs speaking with a lilt and tumble and murmur that was so pleasing. There is a song where Billie Holiday sings "Love is bee-yu-ti-fal" in this birdlike way. There was a Mixtec woman who would show her jewelry, or touch my cheek and say "beautiful" in that same slow way.

We left the next morning. Eager now to get going, because we wanted to come back, to these elegant, gracious, and kind people, to this haunted, dignified place.

An Unnamed Village in Chiapas, Hotel

We renewed our tourist cards at the border. The plan had been to travel in Guatemala, go to the lake, some ruins there. But the rains had begun, Buddy ran out of drugs, the boys all had flu, I thought, but it got worse—dengue.

I drove in rain, on sliding mud; everybody was moaning and throwing up. Finally, we got to a village. I stopped at the first adobe house to ask if there was a place to stay. Both the old man and his wife shook their heads. They said we could stay in their shed until the rains let up and the road was passable. The shed was in the barn, right off the corral. Everything was wet, the rain whipping down now. Cold and wet and new smells, chicken shit, cow shit, horse shit, goat shit. Shed too filthy to sit, just some more space to change David, cut up fabric to clean up everybody, diarrhea and vomiting. Buddy lay curled up and shaking violently on the front seat*

*This final chapter was unfinished at the time of Lucia's death.

The Trouble with All the Houses I've Lived In

Lucia would go on to call eighteen other places home in her lifetime. The following is a list she made in the late 1980s detailing the pitfalls of some of them.

Juneau, Alaska—Avalanche the day I was born, wiped out a third of town.
Deerlodge, Montana—No heat, just the oven. Earthquake.
Helena, Montana—Splinters in the cellar door. Blizzards.
Mullan, Idaho—River right outside, too dangerous to play. Mill right by. Stay inside. Flood.
Sunshine Mine, Idaho—Paper-thin walls. Mama crying crying. Woodstove smoked. Avalanches.
El Paso, Texas—Cockroaches, dark hall, three mean drunks. Drought. Flood.
Patagonia, Arizona—Bats got inside, got scared, batted you in the face. Grasshopper plague.
Santiago, Chile—Maids, day and night. Earthquakes. Two floods.
Rose Street, Albuquerque, New Mexico—Dust storms. Old man died in the apple orchard.

Lead Street, Albuquerque, New Mexico—House Edward Abbey had lived in. Only one burner worked. Filthy.

Mesa Street by the airport, Albuquerque, New Mexico—Airplanes.

Corrales Road, Alameda, New Mexico—No running water, no electricity, no bathroom. Two kids in diapers.

Santa Fe, New Mexico—Acequia Madre ditch. Two kids.

Thirteenth Street, New York City—Five flights up. Two kids, none walking. Blizzard, all streets closed, miracle. Rothko.

Greenwich Street, New York City—No heat after five on weekends. Kids in earmuffs and mittens to go to sleep. I wore gloves to type. Over a ham factory—my W. H. Hudson still smells like ham twenty-five years later.

Fourth son, Daniel, born October 21, 1965

Edith Boulevard, 1966

Acapulco, Mexico—Honeymoon. Three weeks of rain.
 Flood, dysentery, Mark electrocuted, more flood.
Edith Street, Albuquerque, New Mexico—Hard
 water, floor caved in, well went dry. All the
 neighboring ducks came to our swimming pool.
Puerto Vallarta, Mexico—Too many maids, dealers.
 Fear.
Oaxaca, Mexico—Herd of goats next door. Mildew.
 Struck by lightning on Monte Albán.
Yelapa, Mexico—Sharks, scorpions, coconut grove—
 THUD THUD—three kids. Hurricane.
Corrales, New Mexico—Mansion. Three bathrooms.
 Garbage disposal broke, washer broke,
 dishwasher broke. Zinnias wouldn't grow. Roses
 wouldn't grow.
White House, Corrales, New Mexico—Pump broke,
 well went dry, wiring blew, chickens died, rabbits
 died, termites, goat broke leg. Shot her. Rains,
 cellar flooded, bannister caved in, roof fell in.
 New chickens died.

Princeton Street, Albuquerque, New Mexico—Roof fell in. Evicted.

Griegos Road, Albuquerque, New Mexico—I burned it down.

Russell Street, Berkeley, California—Eight people, two bedrooms. Toilet overflowed. Sewer line broke. Evicted.

Telegraph Avenue, Oakland, California—Broken windows. Police all night.

Richmond Street, Oakland, California—Mosquitoes. Police. Fire next door. Evicted.

Alcatraz Avenue, Oakland, California—Crazy landlady. Sirens. Evicted.

Bateman Street, Berkeley, California—Perfect house, garden. Rains, roof fell in.

Sixty-Fifth Street, Oakland, California—Jack in the Box until 2 a.m.

Woodland, California—Heat wave, candles melted, air conditioner broke. R. too paranoid to open

Corrales, New Mexico, 1966

74

Bateman Street, Berkeley, California, 1982

(Photograph by Mark Sarfati)

windows until he threw phone thru window when
I looked at a man on a horse.

Regent Street, Oakland, California—Dark. No light
until night, when the neighbor's floodlight lights
my room, like Soledad. I know it's morning when
it's dark again.

Alcatraz Avenue, Oakland, California—No
catastrophe. So far.

Selected Letters, 1944–1965

November 1944
Overseas

Upson Drive, El Paso, Texas

My Beloved Lucia:

Thanks so very much for the sweet letter. I'm awfully sorry that I haven't written more often. You've been so busy at Radford and there is so little out here to write about except to tell you how very very much I miss seeing your sweet face and listening to your talk and laughter. I think about you and Molly and Mother every minute I'm away and just live for the day I can come home.

So now you're eight years old and you think you like it. Why, you're practically an old woman now, aren't you? Wish I could be there to see you and listen to you tell about your school and your friends and the fun you have. But Daddy is a long way off helping to fight a war to keep the world clean and good for all the Lucias and Mollys in the world.

Many people are being hurt and many dying hoping that this world in which their children are growing up will be the kind of world they wanted for them.

In turn their children will not let them down either. They will grow up fine and honest and good. They will never sneak around doing evil things because they're too fine and proud.

Besides, their hearts would never sing and be happy knowing that they had let filth and ugliness take the place of honesty and goodness. Sometimes it's hard for youngsters to know what is good and what is bad and they must learn as they grow, just as you learn spelling and reading.

There are many things which will teach a person how to grow up beautiful, fine and good. One is the life of Jesus and many, many lovely books which you will read as you grow up. Another teacher is your mother, and another your father. They are there (and I will be . . . one of these days) for you to come to when you are troubled and don't understand anything. But I think the greatest teacher is your own heart. If your heart feels light and airy and you feel like singing, you are being and doing good. If it feels black and soiled and ashamed, you are doing wrong.

The reason I'm writing you this, Lucia, is that I'm so far away I can't talk to you like I used to, and I just suddenly remembered, in the middle of this war, that you're growing up without a daddy, almost. I want you to know, now that you are the young lady of the house, that you are a partner in this family, and we want it to be the most wonderful and happiest family in the whole world and though we may live on a mountain peak one year and in a black canyon the next, that our beautiful house will be built in our hearts. Some great writer said once that lots of gold and beautiful furs could cover many evil things but even rags and dirt couldn't hide a beautiful heart.

I hope you all have a wonderful Christmas and if everything goes well I hope to see you for a short time soon after the first of the year. God bless you, Lucia, and keep you fine and strong and beautiful.

Always your loving
    Daddy

P.S. Kiss Mother and Molly for me.

March 6, 1947
713 Upson Street
El Paso, Texas
(age 11)

Trench Mine, Patagonia, Arizona

Dear Daddy,

I'm sorry that I didn't write sooner but I've been very busy (playin'). We miss you very much.

Geemany Gumpals I have been put in the Low 7th grade because they are doin' fifth grade work in the sixth grade here. I have decided to become a singer because we have so much fun in singing.

How's Mabel? I hear she's your best fren' now. I hope Benny doesn't become a Tom cat. There are so many dog fights here that I don't know what to do.

We went to the symphony today. Miss Buck let us go ahead. We got there so early that we got to go in a drugstore and get a Coke, go to the dimestore, and get to Liberty Hall.

The orchestra was very ugly. They were all mixed up. Instead of putting the violinists in one place, the trombones in one place, and the flutes in one place (one place, one place, ditto etc.) they were all mixed up. And all the men and women had on different colored clothes. The only thing that was good about it was the music, but of course that was the only thing that mattered. We had very good seats.

There aren't very many good shows here now. I saw one *The Red House* that was very good. There was one show that was supposed to be pretty good but I couldn't go and besides I didn't want to. It was called *The Outlaw* but I don't know if it was good or it was dirty.

Just remember that we all love you and miss you very much.

Yours Very Truly and wit' Lot's of Love,

Lucia

Marron Hall, University of New Mexico
Albuquerque, New Mexico
(age 17)

Fort Lewis College, Hesperus, Colorado

Dear Lorna,

Hello you no good wenchy slut . . . I arrived back at school
on the 20th to find quite a few impassioned and resentful letters. We had a band clinic and they invaded Marron, then an
FHA deal so we all had to move for three weeks . . . I won't say
any more as it was bitchy of me not to have written anyway . . .

I would send back the three dollars but you have just saved
my life. I'll send you back the dough next month . . . that made
me mad as I wanted you to come and I invited you. I expected
you to come in August, I was only here a week tho, went to
L.A., had a divine time . . . guess who I went out with, real
big deal . . . Tonto of the *The Lone Ranger* . . . Everybody said
"Oh how wonderful you're going out with Tonto" . . . I died
laughing, his name is Jay anyway . . . My cousin works in TV,
so I really learned a lot about junk, real interesting the sets and
everything . . . The thing I loved the most was *The Lone Ranger*
set . . . A big sort of gymnasium deal . . . with western hotels
and houses and country stores and saloons . . . horses running
all over the place, cowboy extras (divine), manure etc. . . . .
Everything is perfect, down to the spitoon . . . I felt like a little
girl . . . A camera man dropped something and said *mierda*, and
I asked where he had heard it or learned it and it turned out he
had been a sailor and had picked it up in Valpo . . . (diffusion of
cultures) . . . we talked for hours. Everybody was so nice to me
and they all explained things and introduced me to people etc.
My cousin, you remember, the real pretty one, is married (not)
to a guy who is EXACTLY like Danny, only handsome and

tall . . . looks like a stretched out Danny . . . I almost died looking at him and all I did was stare at him.

Oh hell, Lorna, do you have any dough . . . I wish you'd call me and I'll pay you on 1st of Nov. I'm depressed as hell . . . This has never happened to me before . . . I love Lou and we're still going together, but all of a sudden I have become ambitious, and I want to finish school and there are so many bloody things I want to do . . . I never thought school would ever come between me and a guy . . . I'm real proud of myself . . . got two A's in summer school . . . I like this idea of doing something and working for something that I can be proud of doing, you know . . . It would have been out of my Chilean character in S.C. but now I think differently, and I'm scared that maybe it isn't so good. The thought of a refrigerator, deep freeze and grocery bill appalls me (how the hell do you spell it anyway) and I'm worried as hell.

Guess what . . . I'm proctor of Marron Hall, have to crack the whip over all these screaming monsters.

Have you heard from Danny? I dreamt about him last night, with a pink rose in a marine hat. Got a letter from Lionel today . . . I had forgotten all about him and it sure was good to hear from him . . . you know how you love and hate him sometimes, well, I got in a loving mood and wrote a long long letter.

Sonia Lovald has a car . . . she gets more sophisticated every day.

Am taking nineteen hours, Philosophy, Psychology, Russian Novel, Government, Newswriting, Spanish Contemporary Novel, and Art History . . . six term papers in all, so I'm going nuts.

I goofed the other day . . . was depressed as hell and so I opened a charge account, this is why I'm broke . . . I bought a coat on the installment plan . . . I don't know why I did it except that it was the most encouraging thing I've ever done. It's straight down, has real weird sleeves, thin at the bottom, and two big pockets over the boobs . . . I look like an idiot in it but feel real voguish.

Marisol is working at Santiago College . . . can you imagine? I'm sure she's never going to get married. Conchi is going steady with some guy called Jaime Green (I guess you know all this).

Hell, Lorna . . . OH, I forgot to tell you . . . Bernie, Lou's brother, disappeared one morning leaving a note saying he had joined the navy . . . nobody has heard from him since . . . (this was in July). Don Roy, the guy that Irene Barker used to go with, got a divorce, claims to still love Irene. Your old love Mickey asks about the sexy dish from Chile all the time. I haven't seen him tho, but he works in the same building as Lou, who also tries to avoid him. He used to work in the Tribune office but the editor couldn't stand his guts and had him moved to a little room all by himself on the top floor. Tony is OK. He asks about you. You're the only girl I've ever heard him say he liked. Lou said to tell you hello. I love the bastard, Lorna, I really do. I'm just so fouled up with what I want in life or from life, I should say.

We experimented with rats today. Got a rat who was starving to death and who hadn't seen a dame for weeks . . . Well, we gave him two choices, food or the dame . . . and guess what the dirty rat chose . . . the food. The whole point was proof that if we had sex for breakfast lunch and dinner we'd probably all die, and if we thought food was immoral we'd tell dirty jokes about cabbages . . . imagine, a guy saying, "Come on, just one chocolate bar," or "Let's eat artichokes together."

It's almost midnight and I have to get up at six . . . one of my little duties is to stay up (dressed) till 11 and get up at six . . . lock and unlock doors, check rooms . . . I feel like a jailer or a madam, one of the two.

I've got another roommate . . . this one is real nice. Drama major, damn good too. Out of thirty-five girls, twenty of which were seniors, she got the lead in *The Lady's Not for Burning* and she's never been in a play in her life.

Well, my friend . . . I just wrote to tell you that I'm sorry you misunderstood whatever it was you misunderstood, because I miss you like hell, and if I don't write it's because I don't have a damned bit of time.

Please write to me . . . And could you do me a favor . . . send me Johnny K.'s, Alfred H.'s and Martin B.'s addresses? I'm in a mood for them, I miss them all every once in a while, don't you?

Might as well stop before I completely give out.

I love you, Lorna, and I wish you hadn't thought that way about me not writing.

   Love, Lucia

1959 [Spring]
Corrales Road,
Alameda, New Mexico
(*age 22*)

Dorns
501 Camino Sin Nombre
Santa Fe, New Mexico

Dear Ed,

Thank you, really, for your letter, and above all for the poem. You had mentioned what the man said and I have been thinking about it ever since but mostly about how to say everything for the first time . . . not why, which you said in your poem.

You always say all the way YES or NO. It is presumptuous of me to comment on your writing but I know that the Yes and No of it, the evaluation of whatever you are writing about, is

something that Denise and Co. are not concerned with . . .
the commitment and care (caring not carefulness) are what
make you a better writer than they. And is too why I am very
happy that you would read my things. "Well, HE'LL tell you
the truth," Race said, a little sorry for me I think. I hope so, but
also I am glad because I am not so worried about the badness
of the writing itself as about affectation and phoniness which
you are quick to pick up or put down, whatever.

But please, I am so embarrassed and ashamed that you
should speak to me as if I were a colleague. My fault, because
I speak so glibly of my "writing." I know and am sorry, that you
will be very disappointed and shocked by the poorness. Creeley says I am an amateur. But that's all he said, and only when
drunk. Really, I know my writing is bad, that I'm not making
it . . . but I'm not an amateur . . . because I think I could . . . if
only because I have a lot of things I want to tell, to put down
and say. Well.

I have some well said things but they are sent away so I
am sending this poorly said thing. My professor told me it was
the worst thing I have written and this depressed me, for one
thing, because he didn't say WHY. So, I wish you would try . . .
really nothing you could say, not even "I don't like it" would
hurt or discourage me. This is about something that was very
beautiful and valid for me. I want desperately, really, to learn
how to write it that way.

. . . And, Dorns, wasn't that a nice visit? When can you
come to spend a day or so? Race got the job at Bandbox, which
will be nice I think, and has two weeks vacation, so is happy,
especially since his band sounds good, and he is getting tons
of offers for things. Sunday, he plays for Bob Hope show which
should be fun, etc. So everybody here is groovy.

Love, Lucia

Dorns
501 Camino Sin Nombre
Santa Fe, New Mexico

Dear Dorns,

Hey thanks for invitation and Cerrillos job card—a comfort etc. to know they are there, altho I think we're beginning to settle things here in Albuquerque. Race has a job at Western Skies—cinemascope technicolor movie type motel—playing alone, above and beyond the public on a grand piano with a bead curtain around the bandstand. Pay less than Claude's even but hours are crazy—6 to 8 during week—6 to 1 on weekends. Only 2 week contract but maybe it will last—hope so, it is perfect and with more time and calm I think we can settle things here and come to Santa Fe (all of us) to call on you soon. (All this begins next week—now he is working both jobs—I get home from school—Race leaves to rehearse for Bandbox—goes takes shower—goes to Western Skies, Bandbox—and comes home at 2 and goes to sleep.)

I don't know if a vacation to Santa Fe would solve problems or not—I doubt it—my trouble is that I avoid solving them even when they are on top of me—and as I said, maybe as things calm down they will get better. I was feeling very sorry for myself the other day and was pretty unfair. It is such a weakness of my own and such a bloody pattern by this time that I am really frantic about what to do—and at same time I don't want to do anything. I don't want to have to "expect" or demand and it's a big problem with me. I started to work on it with the 80 some pages you have Edw. Hey, I'm sort of embarrassed too about that because I know that if you have not commented it is because you find it hard to do so kindly, etc. So why not let's forget that, OK? It would be less of a task for you and more help to me maybe to deal with less lengthy subjective material. I have some short stories due back next month which are more "polished" and what I want to say is the same as the 80 pages only clearer—it's about moral commitment and as long as I mentioned it—I don't know if I do this badly or what—but it is very hard to write about sex and sort of silly, I think. I tried to in "El Tim" and "Acacia" because it is such an explicit commitment—and I don't think my overall purpose comes thru—judging from Freedman and Ada.

Oh well how did I get on to this—I keep doing such things and tearing up letters to you—it's a hangover from World War II and the business of only writing happy letters. I used to think up, for hours (desperately), anything more or less happy to write my father.

But I'm depressed as hell. School is a nightmare—I'm doing very BADLY—flunked midterm in psych, which is really one of few decent courses I've had in this cheap school. In the other ones I am more or less simply beaten. I just listen and get depressed—not even mad.

Put down mice poison and like this Kafka horrid dream the next few days I had to locate the stench—the rotting horrible stink—all over the bloody house—endless.

33 DEAD BLOATED MICE

And there are at least 3 more somewhere. I can't find them—I just sit and smell them and try and study and go out of my head.

So I took out the poison and threw away the traps and they are scurrying around as ever (almost lost my mind—I mean it). Have you ever worried about flipping?—seriously. Well, I do a lot, so this was encouraging, or maybe I imagined all of it.

Jeffrey and Mark run away together—hide behind the chicken house—lean on each other and giggle while I call them. It's too much—how groovy it is for them now that Jeff walks around. When it's time to go to bed they just go in their room. That's all they do—just walk in—but it is so lovely.

Since the dead mice are in the kitchen and living room, I am in the bedroom and the blind is up four inches because it is so fucking hot and Pete and Co. keep looking in and cursing at me—they know that I have been to court to get them out.

I have been every day for 2 weeks to our LAW (Justice of the Peace) here in Alameda—nothing—they are busy—come back tomorrow—sorry have to go out, see you tomorrow.

I have been six times to plumber's—sure I'll see you tomorrow.

Creeleys came thru. How rested etc. and happy after their vacation. Bob was flipped—gassed—what is a human word—by your writing, Edw.—I mean to the point of definite judgments and statements—not just "too much," which is all I've ever heard him say about anyone.

Liz Okamura much happier in her nice house and more or less a pleasure to be with. I am sorry too I complained about her. I resent anything I have to do with people who depress me and make me feel petty—and as a result bitch about the petty things. Maybe I don't like to be "pushed" or something—I was so bugged by having to help her clean—will gladly do such things when it is my own idea.

Lovely letter from my mother, who ended the letter with being annoyed at having to stop, but the maids had been waiting for half hour to clean her room.

I keep rambling, hoping to suddenly think of something nice to say—or even to ask.

Next week if not sooner we will come pleasantly to see you.

Love, Lucia

1959 [Summer]
Corrales Road,
Alameda, New Mexico

Dorns
501 Camino Sin Nombre
Santa Fe, New Mexico

Dear Edw.,

First to thank you for the help in all the technical adjectives and timing etc., all the things you pointed out to me that were so right, that I didn't know, and no one ever helped me with before. This was the real help I knew I would get from you. I had no idea you would write a letter which would say for me what all writing and art should be. And I, or you, I'm sure, had no idea that you would tell me so clearly exactly what is wrong with my writing and myself. I am completely shaken.

When I was a little girl, not little enough, I wet my pants very conspicuously in the classroom, sort of embarrassing, but to me and all my big girl problems it was too much. I wouldn't go back to school. I refused to go back to school. One day I got a letter saying that I had been appointed a "Safety Sally," one of those kids who wears a halter with a badge on it and stops cars at crosswalks. This was crazy, I thought, and went back to school, wet pants forgotten completely. That I was the only Safety Sally in history ever to patrol the inside of a building prepared for any Mack truck in the world, is beside the point. I think I told you about this, as a sort of funny story, actually it is something that bugs me very much, because it is one of the only positive things I have grasped, to only hide the negative.

Your beautiful letter showed me how much I do this . . . in real life, but mostly in my writing, like the business you mentioned of the two schools. You know I didn't really give much of a damn, except esthetically (?), about the grade school at all. For seven months that odorless skeleton building was my entire fucking life, was the first fucking life I ever had. It was positive, every minute of it, but not one of the positive things was in my story. The parts you liked, the classroom business, this every day was what I worked with, really worked with and loved. There was no "victory" on my part through a dramatic scene with Tim and the nun, although the scene did exist. But there was a victory, an affirmation much more valid than any in my story. It was the difference in Tim and my class and in myself that took seven months of care. This was the first and only time where I honestly forgot myself, the only time I consciously made an effort and a difference for people I loved.

I denied every single bit of this in "El Tim," because of the superficial positiveness, because of my opinions, my vain presence, which were not there in real life. I am so ashamed.

And this false positiveness and this vanity is what screws up the rhythm, because I stop like a little kid passing olives to see if the grown-ups are watching.

Prayers were in English . . . more beautiful because most of the little children didn't know any other English words besides the prayers.

Anyway, I am sick, now chills and fevers from the bang where you got me right in the neck. The neck, where? I don't know. Everybody has always given me a Sally badge, no positive negations ever. I was very shaken . . . I am sure you had no idea what an effect your letter would have.

But the most crazy negative reaction, Edw., is that now I have to rewrite every bloody thing . . . mostly my precious novel which is only a treatise on my positively opinionated self.

Anyway, yes it was a "help." Wow. Thank you.

And Helene, too, for your crazy offer to keep Mark and Jeffrey. I don't think we'll make it tho, but still it's nice. Race is rehearsing every day for two jobs with Prince Bobby Jack and Sonny Coleman . . . remember he talked about Sonny, who is such a fine man and musician. So that's good, I wish you could hear them. Also he's rehearsing with his band . . . they sound crazy. They're young tho and more or less doing this for kicks so I think Race will probably have trouble keeping the whole scene businesslike.

Last night we hit the spots. What a lovely time we had. It's too much, Race on vacation! It was crazy tho, but so weird to go from one place to another, each one was like a Musician's Life—one-act play. Wow, at the Western Skies, a big Hollywood Las Vegas type scene, grand piano and head waiters and rich Texans cursing the band, rich Californians trying to pick up the waitresses. All the time the band is playing together, having this music together, while there is a queer trying to bribe the piano player and a waitress in love with the bass player who is young and the waitress and the queer frighten him. A Cuban is trying to play his guitar and all of the musicians talk about who's playing where and worry about who's trying to get their job (Paul Muench got theirs next week). Ernie Jones plays his guitar. REALLY plays. It was beautiful. At intermission he could hardly stand, couldn't breathe, he is so sick, dying.

We went to the Bandbox, a real niteclub with King and Queen on the restrooms. The owner is a shady character. This was awful, Paul Muench, president of Local 618, was checking cards and told the bandleader he had to stop playing anywhere because he owes so much money to the union. And the bandleader, and the band, could only be bugged at Race, a good friend, who had taken over their job.

Not really, but what else could Chuy, the bandleader, think? He is old and tired, really tired, sitting there playing the drums. Flute player, old Mexican with pan eyebrows who really played. When the show came on a man about 45 with dyed blond hair and sunlamp face got up and begged us to laugh, literally, "Please laugh!" Everybody was too tired. He was horrible. And a girl (sugar-lined) whore, oh well, this scene was too awful, anyway. And Paul Muench told Race's future slimy employer he could break the contract anytime he wanted to.

Then we went to the Hilton "piano bar" . . . all these older traveling men who all at some point said "I am alone, myself" to someone else or to the piano player who is a woman who plays the piano and bitches, just plain bitches in a low voice, like Marlene Dietrich and gossips in a low voice—but she speaks and looks like a lady in a neighborhood, so it is pretty strange.

Then we went to Al Monte's—where Race used to work. That was such a nice place to work—crazy to end there because it is so nice and the people too.

So I don't know when we will come up except for sure next week.

Creeley thru with school and very happy—delightful to be around etc.

Heinz and Bolo in terrible trouble—killing chickens at the head of a gang.

Edw.—I have now 80 pages left of "novel" which are more or less true things. Would you read them? How about Dorn kids on vacation?

Lucia

1959 [Summer]
Corrales Road,
Alameda, New Mexico

Dorns
501 Camino Sin Nombre
Santa Fe, New Mexico

Dear Dorns,

Kept thinking every day we would come the next day—hope Paul OK without blanket. Jean won't give prescriptions for people she hasn't examined but she's leaving in 2 weeks.

93

Before then if you would see her I think she'd give renewable prescriptions and not care about fee. Meanwhile she cleared out her cabinets and gave me a crock of pills—here are all the tranquilizers—one that isn't really labelled is a tranquilizer too and the ones where 3 pink ones are together you take 3 a day and take for several days.

I have:
diaper rash
sleeping pills
diarrhea
suntan
asthma
hay fever
liver pills
(upon request).

Hope you are all OK. I tried to call 3 times but Summers didn't ever answer.

Think we have a house. Really, too, a house (it won't have plumbing for a month!!!) (we won't move in till). It is in the mountains with big stone fireplace and vines and pines and moss and springs and a pond with fish in it. It's crazy, $65 and very big and like a house in Idaho or Montana. Wood with tar-paper shingles and windows that open onto side of hills— too much.

I don't have anything else to say, isn't that fantastic!

Yes, school's out and we have a white cat as of 1 hour ago.

Started a story today. I haven't written (you). I have, but I never can tell if it's true but it's crazy anyway to write to you, know you, etc.

Thank you again for helping me, when you came.

Ernie Jones more or less flipped—beginning that Friday. Started awful fight at Western Skies, got very drunk, wrecked car, broke ribs, and punctured his remaining lung.

It was pretty awful and ironic too, he started it all because he didn't want to die, didn't want to go to hospital, because he was so lonely.

They took him to Bataan Hospital. When Race called to see how he was they told him that Ernie had found out what was wrong with him, left his room, and walked out of the hospital with no lung or ribs and nobody could find him.

And I mean there were 200 people looking for Ernie.

And finally at 2 A.M. they found out he had walked to the Vets hospital and gone back to his old ward. He's better now.

My father sent me the loveliest book, *The Elements of Style* by Strunk (and White, who reintroduced it).

And that's all. Ironically things are OK. I mean they are not so strained and are happy actually but not because they are good but because I've gone all the way—down, in, out, under, out of, terror, etc. Apparently I don't care. The house should help one way or other and the cat, which is crazy—he just wet the bed. He is a $100—blue-eyed—white cat and is neurotic, awkward, dumb, but he's too much—he is like Retie.

Lucia

September 14, 1959
88 Horatio Street
New York, New York
(*postcard*)

Dorns
501 Camino Sin Nombre
Santa Fe, New Mexico

Dear Dorns, Wish we could hear from you—we are on way to Apple—after pretty horrid, painful, wonderful past week—hard + negative + positive + we have met each other + things will be groovy, will be FINE, now.

Love, Lucia

Dear Santa Fe and Helene, Once we got started we figured we might as well keep going. It took just two days is all, not hurrying, so it's not so far. Lucia, when she is not sleeping, is eating, + Marco, baby Jeff + the dog are beside themselves. We'll probably stay here a few days more + then split for the Apple. Everybody says it's hard to find a place big enough so you can come and visit but we'll try.

    Love, Race

1959 [September]
Little Falls, New York

Dorns
501 Camino Sin Nombre
Santa Fe, New Mexico

Dear Dorns,

    Do you know that as we turned onto the road to Race's house we had driven exactly 2,000 miles and we were 20 minutes late—isn't that fantastic—and now I understand it—it is the EAST—where everyone paints their barns on April 2 and mulches their trees on Sept 12 and there is order. Pope said something in a poem about the order in the chaos of nature or vice versa—I am gassed by the richness, TANGLED and matted opulence of the damned nature here—the bloody voluptuousness of rain and grass and snowballs, cosmos, jack-o-lantern, sweet peas, pachysandra, and the order of the restraint people assume in the midst of it. It's too much—and the bloody wasteland in Albuquerque—where people can't take any strength or life from the earth so they give all of theirs up.

    Trip was too much. Jeff was fine, Mark delighted, especially by Indianapolis. Once we had lunch under an ombú tree across from the copper colored sorghum by a watering hole.

The most magnificent thing I ever saw in my life was the MISSISSIPPI at Alton. I felt PATRIOTIC—imagine the settlers and pioneers.

We were efficient until St. Louis (never got a ruddy road map), where we got mixed up and almost made it to Mattoon—we drove all around up there—then later at about 2 A.M. I missed the Ohio through-way and this is the thing about the East—you can't change your mind—you can't screw up, you can't stop.

NO STOPPING

At least in Missouri there were nice signs on one-way streets on the other side thru the rearview mirror that said

TURN BACK NOW

YOU ARE GOING IN

THE WRONG DIRECTION

Anyway, I missed the through-way so we ended up in Cleveland where I got lost in almost dawn on streets above the FACTORIES—brick and fog and smoke and lights. Watch out. Wow.

And you know after going up there so we could drive by Lake Erie—the road was about 50 miles from the lake. We had a glimpse of it, at dawn, from Euclid Ave. in Cleveland.

We got to Race's house on Sunday afternoon. This is the thing I would so love to express, my awe, my complete incomprehension of a real house where birches grow that were planted when each child was born with attics and cellars and summerhouses and all the people in the town have known everyone all their lives and all their relatives and they see each other all the time and like it and speak of birth and death with this fantastic *War and Peace* acceptance. Aunt Fan, showing us her (lovely) house—took us into the study—a real New England paneled study and said "We don't use it much, except for funerals, to put the coats in."

How lovely it was that Race brought me home—that

"Sandy" came home. We are having a vacation and a rest and a honeymoon. Walk down Main St. and through these crazy flowers and grass all over—look thru boxes in the attic—with books and photos and poems by Race and have dinner in dining room with flowers and candles and butter plates and Mark picked corn from a corn field and washed it and ate it. (He is out of his HEAD!) Went to see cousin Andy and his wife Esther and Dorns, these people are TOO much—they work so hard and so easily and mulch (I love that word) and sow and reap and can and prune and graft and darn and bake and plant all their food and everything is so cyclical and ORDERED and NICE—they are all nice—with this crazy wit and an INTEREST in things, everything, and a joy from the views they see every day. I am meeting everyone. They take me in. I don't mean they approve or accept or like me, altho they do, I think, but they take me into their *War and Peace* scene, to their cradles in the attic, and Jeff sleeping in Grandma Proctor's crib that was Bobby's crib too and it's so nice and terrifying. I've never known a family.

I keep thinking of the last family reunion my family had, the children of my grandfather in El Paso and of Mamie, his wife, with big tears in her eyes as she held his coffee cup by the sides while he sat down so he could quick grab it by the handle and drink it down boiling.

That reunion was on Christmas and aside from being a house full of about 30 people there were these things happening. Most of all everyone there was wishing for my aunt to die. She and my uncle had been so bloody happy and in love and fine, all their life, but then she got very sick—really in agony—pain all the time. It was like a reverse Dorian Grey how her body began to destroy her with self-pity and fear and how she began to destroy everyone else. That Christmas Dr. Holt was there, who somehow illegally kept my aunt on cocaine and himself in terrible remorse and horror. My uncle who loved her and watched her and cried at night. Her children who hated her for making my uncle's life so horrible. Her mother, who prayed, was crazy, and who my aunt wouldn't let out of her room not even to eat, only twice a day to go to the bathroom. I was there and it was 2 weeks before my divorce was final and my parents were leaving in 3 weeks. Rex Kipp was there and he is a rich rancher and he and my uncle are best friends. A few days before, he and my uncle had split in a plane and everybody thought they had just gone to get drunk but I found out later they had been preparing for a Santa Claus thing in Mexico where during the night they went to this poor village and put seed and beans and meal and toys and clothes at all the doors. Which is a pretty repulsive Texan thing to do but not really if you think of two drunk millionaires putting around in a plane trying like hell to think of something nice to do, anything nice to do, with their money on Christmas.

Anyway, on Christmas Eve it was cold and there were several things going on—two factions—the drunk ones giving each other deep freezers and TV sets and telling jokes and the religious ones singing the Lord's Prayer and some people cooking hams and turkeys. Poker games and people riding up on new Palominos and everybody had some personal scene—awful violent Faulkner scene going—aside from Christmas Eve, but it was Christmas Eve and my aunt said, "You want me to die, OK, I will," and climbed onto a roof with only a bathrobe on and lay down and it snowed, in El Paso.

There is a crazy thing about my family. If you're going thru a room and meet anyone going thru or sitting, you stop and you touch them, or you contact them—you affirm something—even if often it's some bitter angry thing.

So I can't understand these truly positive people—honest people. Here is the negative portion of my letter and this is what I meant, Edw., when I said I was afraid. I am afraid because I can't make this scene, this nice, so really GOOD HONEST POSITIVE SCENE—where nobody weeps or screams or curses or hugs or fucks up or despairs or desires or kids themselves or dreams. Like the Newtons, truly so kind and they love Sandy (Race), very much—but when they saw him they said, "Why, hello Sanford!" But no weeping. When cousin Andy came back from the war half-dead, after horrible time, his father shook his hand. "Hello, Andrew." Nobody is CORNY here.

And so corniness ultimately unimportant and superficial—the dependability and strength of love is here. Ah. But once when I was very little I dug Frost and "Stopping by Woods" and then I read "The Death of the Hired Man" and there is a line there that says (more or less) "Home is where, if you haven't anywhere else to go, they have to take you in."

I wish I had my damn typewriter—I want to write—which is crazy. I suddenly have 100s of things to write—but anyway the second day we were in Little Falls, in that lovely place, THE WELL RAN DRY! No water! First time in 60 years.

So we came to Hatch Lake—TO SHADYSIDE where SANDY GREW UP—A CRAZY LAKE and CRAZY (real) CABIN and we are camping, washing selves and clothes in the lake and Mark and Jeff delirious. Crayfish and snails and water snakes and squirrels and chickadees—we lie down in bed and see tons of trees and the sky and if you sit up against the pillow you look down on the lake. Right now we are at the dock and Jeff is throwing rocks and snails in the water. Race is reading (he has 100s of crazy books here), I am in a boat with a cat, and Heinz is tormenting us. Mark's asleep in Grandma Proctor's iron bed.

Last nite Aunt Moe, who lives next door, came to dinner with Race's mother and father and Dana, his brother and Lee, Dana's wife, and their children, and we had corn (you put the water on—then run and pick corn, quick dump it in, cover it with husks—cook for 3 min. and eat). We ate out on porch over lake on old chairs with oil cloth on table and it was nice and fun. Aunt Moe is as lovely a lady as I had imagined (she's the box and paper lady). We had a good talk while we boiled water in crazy kettles and washed dishes and cut glass jelly bowls.

I'm getting seasick. Mark and Jeff are FAT and browning. I AM FAT—can't button that blue dress I had in Santa Fe over me at all, in fact I am suddenly wholesome as hell—fat and no makeup (first time in 10 years) and tired from rowing and reaching across big old beds to make them.

Hey and the main reason I'm writing is that Race's father, when we ran out of water, called Mr. Jay Murphy, who is a
                              DOUSER
who came in these crazy grey overalls with his alder stick and started stomping thru the woods and found where 3 veins of water met.

He gave me the stick and had me walk toward where the water was and I did and nothing happened. We did it again and he took one end of the Y and I took another—just barely holding it. He took my hand and as we got closer the end started to pull downwards—to be PULLED by the EARTH.

He said it didn't matter what kind of a stick he used—that he could do it with wire, even, because it was the GIFT, his gift that mattered. "I don't know why. I just know."

Dr. Newton tested him by asking him to try it in places where he (Dr.) knew exactly where the vein was, and Mr. Murphy got it absolutely right. It was so damned far out, his hands so EASTERN and SO OLD.

Ee-ah, they say, instead of yeah or OK.

Aunt Moe has the gift of dousing too and I can see it—she has will. Didn't we speak of this, Edw.? WILL, that is what people have here—somewhere it should relate to faith, like Melville's, or to passion, somewhere it could, could be power—

like Melville—because it is strength—but there is the order, the order of Melville's "I and My Chimney."

Now we are on the porch. I'm on a silly old chair by a pillow, with faded brown needlepoint that says:

LOOK UP AND NOT DOWN
LOOK FORWARD AND NOT BACK
LOOK OUT AND NOT IN

I keep beginning to end this illegible letter—but to end I always want to say something about leaving you and knowing you—we miss you. This is what's left, like my uncle said, how we are friends.

Love, Lucia

P.S. Mark got in a rowboat all by himself—lugged the oars up and into the slot deal and rowed perfectly, except that boat was moored or anchored or whatever. He is radiant, beautiful.

My story came back from Kerouac. Said it was the wrong address—is it Rhode Island or Long Island?

1959 [September]
Little Falls, New York

Dorns
501 Camino Sin Nombre
Santa Fe, New Mexico

Ee-ah, but I try to reread my letter and there it is—but just barely because ultimately I'm so confident and happy—but it's there—the shrill positivism. So let me say two things in my new campaign for it. One is that when I sit on top of the hill by the summer house where it is so quiet—thick and cushioned with grass and flowers, and it's still. Where everything is green and beautiful and you can't see the sky except when the wind blows—well this is it, there is no sound and there is no light.

I feel awkward not being sure of the sky and to be facetious, but not really—you can't see the river for the trees.

Remembered the day we moved into Alameda and we were washing dishes by the pump in the sun. Hell, I miss sitting on the steps when it is going down, with Buddy.

Buddy called on Monday—a typically horrid thing to do—he knew Aunt Fan and Aunt Moe and Aunt Reba and Cousin Betsy would be in the parlor by the phone, that Race would be there and that it would upset me and that it would make me happy to hear him—and this is the thing—it is so EASY for us to know how to touch each other or to hurt each other. I hurt him over the phone, he was crying—but the thing is that I did it not because I want him to simply go away—but because I was angry because he called, and angry, hurt, about the "broad is a broad" thing, which he said, even tho he said he didn't. He said it because he was angry, knew it would hurt me. Isn't this horrid—but it is so easy, the tenderness, and this is it.

Oh hell—this is complicated and I don't know how to say it.

It's like the difference between being drunk and being doped that we talked about.

The ultimate value of a drunken self—like me and Race—so awkward and clumsy but with it, trying to make a life—like trying to pick up a petal when you are drunk. This is worthwhile and positive.

I believe in this—it is so unnatural to me—it is hard.

Love, Lucia

1959 [Fall]
106 West 13th Street,
New York, New York

Dorns
501 Camino Sin Nombre
Santa Fe, New Mexico

Dear Dorns,

Hey, 1st of all, since letters are so groovy because only one person can talk at a time, it's really crazy to have left and heard from you, Helene, such a nice long letter and crazy to have got it the day we moved into our new house on

106 W. 13th, NY, NY

Wow—we were worried too and for a while it was all very discouraging—car broke down several times ($$$$) and what with things like $100 deposit to get a phone, $300 deposit to move into a $100 a month apt. half as big and twice as beat as our house in Alameda, plus having no $ at all—it was pretty frightening. Every place we looked at was depressing, horrid, and expensive. There was one that was possible—$300 to move in, then only $65 a month. One big room, a hot plate, one window at one end and bath in the kitchen or vice versa—but it had a fireplace and was sort of jazzy—on Cornelia St., but couldn't make the naturalism and poetic suffering of it even tho it was in throbbing heart of Village etc. So, anyway, we have a pretty crazy pad—I mean it is nice, up 4 flights of stairs and it is in back and is quiet with big windows in every room and a real kitchen (more or less) but it is LIGHT and sunny and there is a bay type window in one room that looks down and out on trees and everybody's gardens in backyard. The street is nice, too, very Henry Jamesish with trees and window boxes and no delinquents, just old gentlemen and very old ladies. Anyway, it is nice and right now I'm on our bed and I see all these crazy minaret and parapet chimneys, and absolutely all I can hear since it's Sunday are birds and buses and bells and I'm not trying to be alliterate but that's all I hear, except Mark and Jeff, who are in their room and it's sort of nice because they have their own sunny room, and are in it (barricaded) but can see us etc.

Race is in Little Falls picking up the piano—next thing is to get piano fixed up. The next thing is for me to get a job for 3 months, which shouldn't be hard, I don't think. I might get something with Grace Lines, since I speak Spanish and half of its passengers don't speak English, and I know all the presidents and vice presidents. Then the next thing is for Race to get job which seems hard, seems harder to him, but I am very confident and it may take time, but in the job and music aspect, wow, I think this was the best move to have made, ultimately. Race plays better than 90% of piano players here—and the other 10% —how crazy (good and bad) that they are here working and playing at all—except that Bill Evans and Red Garland and Jaki Byard are all playing RIGHT NOW in N.Y. and we are too broke to go—or to Miles Davis, also here—very frustrating! But they are RIGHT HERE.

Yes, Edw., it was the best move—it really was. I didn't know this, know it and believe it, when we left Albuquerque, or even when we got to Little Falls—because we hadn't yet moved, ourselves, closer or higher or further—toward anything or each other.

And actually it was even worse for a while—it was as awful as it could be because we had done it, moved and agreed, and things were not better. I did not understand—I still was not trying to understand—why we were in Little Falls and felt as if I was not a part of Race's life or what everyone there believed in—but it was because I'm still having trouble thinking of anything but myself. It wasn't until I started to see Race coming from that life and from his family and from the trees and the lake that I began to understand him.

I was still pretty sick—I mean sick, like an illness, my masochism, which is like dope, the extreme of masochism-suicide, a denial—and I didn't know then (honestly) that that was what Buddy was—everything that I hate—suicide like the snakes that devour each other. I don't know what I wanted more, to destroy or to be swallowed—but I didn't know this, I didn't see how horrible I was—then I did, in myself. I'm trying not to say anything anymore that I am not sure is the truth.

Anyway, I feel like I have been very ill, and now I'm well and I'm tired and glad I'm well. Happy like you are when you are tired and glad. I don't think I am capable anymore of my false exhaltance, false positivism, I'm too tired and glad—and yes, again, this was the correct move.

We are walking and talking and laughing and fighting and worrying and getting mad and depressed and excited. It's very crazy and good. And no matter what finally happens, we will have done this together, and worked at this—N.Y., at something.

And it is TOO much, N.Y. Everything. We have been all the hell over it. It is VAST. I mean vast. All these people LIVE in it, in every block and they are all going upstairs or downstairs or in or out and they are all a part of a block, a whole endless block with delicatessens and shoe stores and people going upstairs and downstairs.

Subways are crazy because you come up into a new world and it is as if the place you have been isn't there anymore at all—which is crazy but I don't like it, it's just like airplanes—you don't go from one place to another, you simply eliminate the first place.

But the buses are too much—how many hundreds of worlds and districts and parks and S. Klein's and people you have to go thru to get to our house. And you could keep going thru millions of different others if you wanted to.

Hey Helene—that crazy black sweater you gave to Jeff—

Maggie° and I have capitalized on it. We're starting a Home Industry—children's sweaters and ponchos—borrowing $50 to put an ad in Westchester papers—people send $10, we buy $2 of wool and make it and send it and our business will begin to mushroom. I love that expression, since I saw mushrooms mushrooming in Little Falls.

Yes we went to Goodman's—we had been hectic and nervous and worried about place to live and money and had talked with some friends who were older members of Beat Generation and it was pretty depressing. When we went into their (Goodman's) house, Jeff went over to Mitch, leaned on him, and smiled and almost fell asleep and that's the way I felt—it was so calm and we sat around and talked and laughed—too much, just sitting around. Mitch is lovely—such a warm strong person—Denise was a good surprise in every way—much nicer than I had imagined, much less complicated and also nice to be around and talk with. She's very efficient, which was not a surprise. I wonder at her attitude toward their son—they don't leave him at night because the building might catch on fire—but otherwise she seems pretty quiet about things—not insistent—which is a pleasure. If there is anything I hate it's insistence!

Now I am sitting in our window looking at the trees and there are some morning glories on a trellis.

Mark and Jeff really like it here—Mark just because of the boats and trains and other conveyances. He really dug the country and trees and water—was so happy there—but Jeff is a rake, a dandy and N.Y. is his—he seriously believes that the whole scene is for his benefit and is very appreciative and gracious—like Castro from a convertible, he waves and shouts, acknowledging the lights and buildings and pigeons and noise.

°Our friend who lives on Horatio (all of us in one room for 2 weeks and it was fine). She is a lovely lady, funny and warm and kind. You would like her.

What torture your letter of green chilis and piñon nuts! Oh, Ai—the other day I was walking—we never used to walk very much, Race and I, in the country—it's too much, walking—and I passed by a frozen food plant on a little street and smelled a groovy smell and went inside. Lo and behold, some lady was making 1000s of empanadas with refried beans—so I bought some and they were groovy, only there wasn't any chili on it.

But the delicatessens and Hero sandwiches—I am going out of my head, so much good food everywhere.

Martinson's Coffee is 83 cents and we think of you, drinking it.

We think of you all a great lot actually. Please write.

Greenwich Village—too much—like Claude's, spilling out onto the streets and into cellars with burlap café curtains. But the people, the ponytailed ones and ivy league haircutted men in bulky olive green sweaters—they are young and so hopeful. It's nice.

Except for the little toy dogs—little poodles and chihuahuas and big weimaraners awful awful. They crap in the street while their owner, not master, waits. Poor dogs, what an indignity to shit in the street.

Heinz—oh that was awful until we went back to Little Falls to get our things and saw him—he is exactly where he should be, guarding a manor-type place rustling around in leaves (It's Autumn!) and barking and carrying on. The tradespeople are terrified of him. Race's mother gives him constant attention which he also likes and eggs and steak and chicken livers and broth and stew and chocolate cream cookies and SNACKS all day. He is FAT and shining—looks beautiful and happy.

How about that worthless POT! I should have known—Bobbie Creeley told me it was "extremely valuable." She also told me that the rat poison had a built-in chemical that made the mice all go outside and die and not smell.

Your job sounds good, Edw.—you like it? What are you writing? Isn't autumn in Santa Fe fantastic?

I think I'd better wait to write until something happens to tell you, otherwise I will just go on and on. Wish you were all here—we could walk around and go to the pier and DIG things and talk and laugh.

—Love, Lucia

P.S. Mark uses his fist for a phone and calls Fred and Paul and Chanee and then he takes them out of the phone and plays with them. How about TV! Don't you like *Rawhide*—Mr. Favor is so good and moral and strong. Mark on the trip, looking out of the back window, kept turning dials pretending to watch television.

1959 [November]
106 West 13th Street,
New York, New York

Dorns
501 Camino Sin Nombre
Santa Fe, New Mexico

Dear Dorns,

How about the chocolate! It is crazy—all wrapped up like a Hershey and then you open it and it's Mexican crumbly and good—we drank it on a rainy nite. It's raining here now, drizzling and downpouring—not today but in general. Today is Sunday, shining like a Fred Astaire movie—Marco and Jeff and I walked for blocks, a GAS. Pigeons and a cat sitting in a bowl and the weird selection of people who are up on Sunday morning—especially this morning since it's daylight savings time but M & J don't know it yet and are up at 6. Race came home from playing about 7:30 with a Sunday paper and CHEESE DANISHES.

Pretty groovy. We're relaxing with all the excitement. I DIG N.Y. Really do, after decay and old dying dust of Albuquerque, even the greed and aggressiveness is refreshing.

The wariness is only thing that bugs me—count your change—everyone does that in every way—I see it in everyone here, even the Goodmans, with their friends, let me see your hand first. It's so much more (positive) to accept or reject all the way, even if you're wrong.

Home Industry is making it. $90 in one week ($45 each), which is very groovy, since we have orders for more stoles and ponchos and 50 men's velvet bathrobes (!!!!) and A CAPE, and it is a GAS, to have somebody say design and make a CAPE.

Sewing time is almost nothing and buying time is FUN. I love the stores and storerooms. It has become such a pleasure for me, looking for fabrics—I dig it—the cloth and weaves and colors—the whole scene. Mr. Astrid who saves little pieces, short ends, just to be nice, but still bitches and haggles over the price. Our main retail outlet (!) is GLAD RAGS—a real L.A. type store—jazzy—but not the sophisticated, polished N.Y. jazz—sort of vulgar and pretentious. Marty owns it, and where Santa Fe is run by Claude's Margaret, Greenwich Village is run by Martys. Caricatures of virility. Magnificent-looking men who fling off their mohair sweaters. "Never was my type, it's rather cheap." He's OK tho, very straight—not much polish etc.—gives us $7.50 for stoles, sells them for $15—but we make $5 so everybody is happy—except his young partner in his mohair sweater who thinks all stoles are cheap and all women are cheap. "Isn't there something rather cheap," he says, hanging up some Continental corduroy trousers, "about men who will let themselves have a 34-inch waist?" His name is A. Pompeii, that's how he signs our orders.

Except for dealing with him, everything is groovy. Most of all because our products are truly nice and pretty. What a ball to walk down street and see them in shop windows.

Hey, I'm glad you met Vlahos. Say hello to him. How do you like job? Sounds very good—in spite of jaded and electric eyes. What of the Nebraska thing?

Max Finstein asked for your address. Apparently many people here have been hearing your taped poems. Max has "contacts" with Noonday—wants to have some of your poems. He's writing to you anyway.

I'm having lunch with my agent next week. I wish the day wouldn't come. I think it is so funny to say "I'm having lunch . . ." I mean it really is.

Was learning how to be a Fashion Model from friend of Denise & Mitch. They think I could make it but doubt if I'll do it. It is a real Stanislavsky Art. First you believe you are a magnificent, conceited, arrogant, elegant Bitch and when you feel this way your cheeks suck in and your neck juts out and your shoulders drop and your pelvis slouches and your toes point and your umbrella gestures and you look like this:

and they say "Perfect! Hold it," for half an hour.

Wish you, both, all, would write.

Love, Lucia

P.S. Did you ever read *A High Wind in Jamaica* (*The Innocent Voyage*). It's crazy. He writes about tons of things happening at once or in a sequence like nobody ever could. It is too much, if one is a parent, to read it.

1959 [November]
106 West 13th Street,
New York, New York

Dorns
501 Camino Sin Nombre
Santa Fe, New Mexico

Hi Dorns— Today we went for a walk—Race is gone and we are aimless. Nothing for us to do but hang around. I MISS him so we walk in spite of the rain and today we went to Lower East Side and with the rain and being aimless it was very sad and depressing. Soggy pushcarts.

We came back tired, so tired we stopped to rest, in a restaurant.

Sat down at a table and waited politely. An elderly man in black with silver hair and foreign accent came up and said,

"What is it you wish?"

"Coffee with cream. Two milks, no, one milk and two glasses, and some kind of donuts."

"Blueberry muffins?"

"Yes, fine, thank you," I said.

He came back with a tray and poured the milks, undid the paper from around the muffins, lit my cigarette, and said, "That will be forty cents." All I had was 50 so I gave it to him murmuring, "Keep the change."

"Thank you," he said.

"Thank you," I said, and he went over to another table, picked up his umbrella and put on a bowler hat and left, bowing to us. We were in a cafeteria!

Flower stores are pushing wheat, orange berries, yellow and brown mums, and deep rust asters and in the back are these gentle violet spring flowers. They are heather. Have you ever seen HEATHER?

Race wrote, such a crazy letter, and it sounds good, his gig, if only because it is such a GAS. They broadcast every night from the Persian Terrace of the Syracuse Hotel with 4 trombones playing "Shine on Harvest Moon" and those revolving domes of broken mirrors in the middle of the ballroom. Ferns.

A customer dug one of the capes in our major retail outlet so much she ordered 2 more—which was crazy—altho last 2 checks from major retail outlet bounced, leaving us hung for $90. He's going bankrupt. He paid for last order by trading for a suit with a fur collar—just like Proust's.

What about Nebraska and the long-named lady? What's happening? Hey H., it would be groovy to get another long letter.

Mark calls you all the time, you five and Mary Lou and Lourdes and LeRoy and Pete. They are the people I miss too.

I can't think of anything else to say!

    Love, Lucia

                       February 5, 1960
                       106 West 13th Street,
                     New York, New York

Dorns
501 Camino Sin Nombre
Santa Fe, New Mexico

Dear Helene,

Keep waiting for spirits enough to write you a letter, don't come so I will just tell you how fine it was to get your good letter, to hear about your happy birthday and the birds, and (damn!) New Mexico, that sounds pretty good nonetheless. Hey, it is really great that you know about sleet storms. How come we never talked about them? The drawing of Fred, I love very much the way it is done, clear and lightly and with all of his tenderness, like when he looks as if he were just going to cry or to laugh. I miss them, we all miss your children very much.

I would like to talk to you, with you. Things here not so very good at all. No work and we have been living on unemployment. Race is very worried and tense. It is taking all of the little strength I have, it's as if this is the last play I can make, to make it by trying not to be petty, not to feel guilty or put down or jealous or inadequate. What have I been doing, fucking around all my life? It was only a few months ago, maybe weeks, that I began to learn about loving, about love. Now I'm suddenly understanding marriage and how lightly I treated it, and how hard it is (and simple).

There is a lot of pettiness around here. Lots and lots of downright cutthroat badness, mostly in the gig scene, but mostly pettiness. For a while it seemed that it was all revolving around Creeley, that everyone was dropping his name and their grievances. And suddenly I realized that I had done so too. Once when I was very little in the Grand Canyon there was a waitress with a huge tray of coffee in cups walking across the restaurant. One of the cups fell and smashed on the floor and she sort of looked up at heaven and said oh hell and tossed the whole tray onto the floor and split. That is what I do all the time. I felt so sorry for having said anything about Bob behind his back that I decided to say it to his face. So I wrote a horrid letter with all the awful things I could think of, and as you know, I could support none of them. I hurt him badly and disgusted him and myself. I think I more or less learned something else. I could think all those things about Bob, but never did they ever have anything to do with who he was, the very fine things that I respect in him and love him for. I had not realized how simple it is to destroy things. I keep trying to think of that thing of a man is his deeds and that this is not true. In a way, the point is which of the deeds are the man. Damn, I swore never to write you a bugged letter. But that is mostly what I am thinking about.

Spent the morning, a balmy day, with the Goodmans, and

it was very great. Somehow a lot of the time we had talked about personal things, it's impossible to be straight or personal about things. Yesterday was very groovy, everybody was finding how many things there were to dig and see and hear about. It was very nice and happy.

Spend a lot of time in this secondhand bookstore, The Blue Faun, where I found *The Purple Land*, and where I am trying to find the autobiography. "It's light blue and torn on the bottom," the guy says. He can't see . . . hardly at all and knows all the books by the cover. He has an opinion about all of them, and everything, and I found out because he insisted that I buy his book. He is Guerney, the Russian translator. "They are beginning to rediscover me again." Now I can see why Nabokov can say he is the only translator of Russian . . . because he is a boor. A buffoon. He is exactly like father Karamazov. He is probably the most literal person I have ever known, he boasts of translating Lorca without knowing a word of Spanish etc. I am impressed and it is nice because it is such a good example of what we were discussing about translators. And it isn't even to get the "spirit" in addition to the words, this guy does that very well, I am sure. His grand inquisitor gives a much more blunt and "Russian" type sense, but it is not beautiful. He is pretty great to talk to, tho. He is conceited and dogmatic and stomps his foot and is ridiculous, and here is the deed thing too. God, he loves to read, he loves Russian and the things he translates, and the books he pushes . . . "If you like Hudson you'll like this, buy this . . . No, oh what a fool!" he says and he is actually very sad and upset.

The poems are of course translations. And as for the novel, they paid a down payment on an option for the pages (once revised for the ninetieth time) of the one you had. They have read it but not as an "official" submission, since the ruddy thing isn't finished and I hate it and maybe never will. But anyway, they dig it and say they will buy it, so why don't I finish it or submit a complete enough outline ending and enough pages, so they can give me another advance. They and the agent keep writing about when we're going to have lunch to talk about it, since it is a real cinemascope Tab Hunter on a horse in the wind type scene, about movie rights etc. I am back to where I started with it, and don't want to send them more, even for the damn money, because at this point, that's all I would send it for. So I'm starting it over, adding to almost every page. The nice thing is that most of the stuff that's down I dig very much. The sad thing is that I wrote it when I was, well hell, yes, when I had a hell of a lot of joy in my ruddy heart, when I could write about all these characters and really feel kind toward them and care about what they would be doing in the next paragraph or how they would think something was funny or beautiful. Now when I try to go on with it I can't do it. I have looked at myself for too long. So I'm looking around, trying to, and as I said, it is very hard to do it straight in the eye.

I saw *Children of Paradise*, did you?

Love, Lucia

February 6, 1960
106 West 13th Street,
New York, New York

Dorns
501 Camino Sin Nombre
Santa Fe, New Mexico

Dear Edw.,

The past few weeks I have written so many letters—some of them unfortunately I sent but can't remember if I told you how great it was to get the poem. We both really dug it. Delicately sure—beautiful.

Love, Lucia

•

Dear Ed,

I would like very badly to talk to you. I think of you with a visual image, of clarity.

Honesty and all that jazz. How to be, I wish to be flippant now. Here, this is what has happened—Little, Brown and I are signing a contract—$250 to have first option on my novel—which they haven't read, only five stories—$250 is to read it and publish the whole thing if they want (for $1000s or something more). If they don't want it, I get to keep $125 (half) anyway.

I am so miserable. I have never been so afraid and unhappy—maybe you will see why. One is the mercantile ring of it—the business deal (which is a gas) with my stories, but with my novel it hurts that they should pay even before reading. Even before it is written. The other is that I am committed now to write it and I am afraid. I reread what I have done so far and read it in terms of what I think other people would like and I hate it, and reading it in terms of what I wish I had been able to say, I hate it even more.

This is what I have so longed for. A receipt—an acceptance, a justification—"I am a writer." I am so ashamed. I forgot about the writing. But more than that—it's as if I had been insisting that I was, even in my apologetic way, and now I have been taken up on it. Ed, do you see, it is a glorious thing, the permission for a commitment, in myself. Please understand this, that now I have to admit to myself that this is what I am going to do, all the way.

I'm completely incoherent. Nothing ever has hit me quite so hard, morally. Because you see, I believe, as I once wrote to you, that I am a writer, that I am not an amateur. I even believe that I am a good one. But the fact that I was not proud of anything I had done was unimportant, the writing was the important part. Now something has been demanded of me—now I must demand something of myself, my writing.

Oh, can you possibly see how marvelous and terrifying this is for me? I never had the faith, to write as an artist, as a writer must, to simply write, because I am too vain. Now that someone else has said, OK, you are a writer, I must begin at the beginning with the FAITH. I have to begin. Oh gosh, goddamn I wish you both were here. Race is on way to Syracuse again and I won't be able to call him for 2 days. Goodmans don't like me, Maggie likes $ and would simply think it crazy and would not see what is happening. I hope you do.

Ed, do you see why I am ashamed? That it was so easy for me. Everything is always easy for me, not inside of me—but in anything that I want. I am ashamed because I know that I could have made it more difficult for myself. I could have been a writer, but it would have been too hard to care more about what I saw and how I said it, than what I felt, what I was. I have to do this now, in order to feel that I am not cheating, to justify the EASE.

Does any of this make sense?

Here, I have spent 8 pages, all I should have said was that the proof and the praise that I thought was all I needed, doesn't work. I am still not proud and I am not yet humble. Those are the things I want, that one has to have.

—Please write.

Love, Lucia

106 West 13th Street,
New York, New York

Dorns
501 Camino Sin Nombre
Santa Fe, New Mexico

Dear Helene,

Thank you for the "goddamn sermon," for your very beautiful letter to me. I have, we have, been "straight" since the manic-panic time when I wrote to you. I almost believe it won't happen again—that I will complicate things—but if I ever start tinkering, I'll read your letter. I will anyway, for it was very fine.

Ai—it is "hard" and a "thing" for me, marriage and love, because when I "learned about love," only since we have come here, it was simply that for the first time in my LIFE, I was not doing love. Love had always been a task for me, not a "duty" but a thing of deeds, to show to parents etc., to do what they wanted me to do, and of roles to act out, with them and others and mostly with Paul. I had never known it to be otherwise. It is so "hard" not to connect love and care for someone else's happiness with a feeling of having to do (any) specific things and most of all with the fear that whatever it is I should do, I will fail.

But this is so rare now. I'm sorry I wrote to you when I was feeling this way—it is a sin. Was what I meant long ago by selfishness and by guilt—how to stop imposing things upon myself, to get out of myself and just be. Do you know, Helene, that I never had been this in my life until recently, I had never let anyone be this with me. Can you understand the happiness it has been for me, and for Race too, but still that it is "hard" to accept, to give assent.

OK, cross my heart, last last of my problems, etc.

We are laughing now, in debt and broke and sickly and it rains, rains and we drink the Mexican chocolate and listen to the wireless, glassy-eyed. The trio has a job in Queens, which is a relief and a delight since it is a jazz gig, adding a good saxophone player. We made a pact for the 90th time, to remember not to get low.

Everything is so bloody relative and silly—like, we have big, fat supercilious dapper mice and they are great!

Another big, fat pressure off my reeling head, so now there are none, was that I finally had a meeting with Little, Brown, with "Oh, do call me Peter," actually, and Volkening.

If I have said anything good about Volkening recently, like, FORGET IT. He is an agent. Namely, I had not understood what that meant. He is a goddamn pimp.

Anyway, we had a literary luncheon. In case you're not hip this means 6 (stiff) drinks and lunch at Hotel Algonquin.

Volkening had 8 bourbons and sat around trying to keep me from saying anything so he could tell "Do call me Peter" what I was going to write. Oh, I can't even tell, it was so ridiculous. I will tell only that, as I was peeing in the ladies room, he continued a deal for an advance of 500 beans for 50 pages more and while he went to the men's room, I said to Peter I wouldn't take it, I didn't like the ruddy book and I wanted to start all over, and if they liked it OK, if not OK. Actually the guy was very sweet and stupid and decent and was so impressed by my "quiet modesty" (that's how he talks, I have "silver prose" I'll have you know), that he said just to send 100 new PAGES. Why the fuck not pounds or feet? I write lovely pounds. Jesus, and they would almost certainly buy it outright.

It was pretty awful. Volkening was mad about $ and because I said I didn't know what I wanted to do with the book at all and he was mad because somehow the whole thing was between me and the editor (the damn guy read it 3 times, E for Effort, and sincerely dug many things, and while V. was out, admitted that it was lousy as a novel, but he can't risk losing Volkening, you see).

Anyway, he, Peter, grew up on a farm in Colorado and is a weak would-be idealist, and as we took leave of him, there in the lobby he murmured how I was as lovely as my writing, and Volkening muttered, "Well, you've cinched that, honey."

The only move short of kicking him into the palm pot was simply to say to hell with him, which I easily did and no longer feel any debt to him or Peter, etc. I went to his office and took back my old man and the apples story. I love that story very much—the others are pages, he can pimp for them.

And I feel great—maybe I'll never write another word for the rest of my life, maybe I will. That, too, will never be a task again.

I am reading Hardy. He is a fine man too, and his sense of place—don't you dig him?

Race is reading Zen and learning Chinese. He is the only person in western world I know in whom this would not be an affectation.

We are both so glad for knowing the Goodmans, that they are here in this city and for Max, who is great. He and Rena were here this afternoon and it was very crazy. She is pretty insistently maternal about (not with) children, which is a drag, but is very quiet and otherwise nice.

Denise is great and great too about turning people on, a lovely trait, like calling up tons of people to go and see someone's painting that she saw and liked. I have read many things I would not have known of or loved—except Virginia Woolf, who I don't dig at all.

Saw Peter Orlovsky in a hunting cap in front of the tigers in Museum of Natural History. We went with Nick, and lost him. It was pretty scary (and funny) searching for him thru elephants and gorillas. Jeff was gassed. Marko not at all because it was all fake, he was even a little mad. We all dug the birds tho.

They have Feelies now in N.Y. Something on the seats in movies, so you feel all the sensations on the screen and you can even attack and strike back.

Guerney is too much—he doesn't even know me unless I go in with M & J, he can tell us by our shapes, otherwise he tells me the exact same things. He is a naïve REAL Rebel, like all by himself. I like him.

It's Sunday now—we're going to Abingdon Square so Race and the lady downstairs can sleep. She is foreign, very polite considering that "they go skipping, skipping and only on Sundays."

Thank you H. for your letter, etc. Write, both. Is it Spring there?

Love, Lucia

P.S. Robins! It seems impossible.

1960 [November]
277 Greenwich Street,
New York, New York

Dorns
Pocatello, Idaho

Dear Edw.,

"Shit, you so much don't care about all this."

You are very wrong. My fault. I have left myself wide open.

I care about a ruddy lot of things—including my writing. True, it is a matter of commitment—this is where I am hung— this is what my "guilt" is—that it is hard for me to commit myself (to writing, love, god, etc.). I keep hoping people will help, hoped something like Little, Brown would help. It did only in that I saw it can't. I simply imagined that you would see that, the main point, not come on with a letter about money and art.

OK, and your paraphrasing sarcastic "you, who do things so easily." I did not say that. I said things come easily to me, for me. I would like for things to be hard, I would like to be asked to commit myself. It is no help to be paid for something that hasn't been read, perhaps won't be.

Your letter for "El Tim" was the most help, demand, I have ever had. "You so much don't care." I am naive, I don't understand how you can call me your friend.

Modesty and humility are not at all the same. I do not want modesty, I don't even like it. Humility implies respect for something else.

I had a birthday. Maybe I came of age. Altogether, that day a letter came from my agent—the bastard who came on like Papa Bear to hook me—and now he can say—in answer to the letter that I didn't want to sign until they had read it. Forget it, sign—put your face on the book jacket and you'll sell a million copies. Things come easily for me. And then a letter from my mother, who forgot my birthday, but remembered to tell me how I have never been anything but a disappointment to them. I told her to go to hell, in a letter, and in my heart. I too am sick and tired of guilt. Formal dismissal came, I "haven't been worth the worry and heartache" I caused them. OK, it hasn't been worth it trying not to.

Jesus, I am sad. Also, that day my pocket was picked, 40 dollars.

Race didn't write after the first week, had nothing to say and spent weekends at his parents. One night, a pretty dam cold N.Y. night, I was feeling despair. I was sad. I am only sad now, but I felt self-pity, ugliness, and the phone rang, and it was Buddy. I could have felt terror, I suppose—at his circling, hovering for my soul—but he was there, he touched my head, it was good to hear him.

Bought a desk, to get it went up to sixth floor beat hole where a family had fled leaving behind everything including

Mary Rose Saliba's toys, a peanut butter sandwich and milk glass. In the desk, when I got home, were 25 of her notebooks from the beginning of the second grade to the end—arithmetic, she was very good, mostly Catechism—but even with all the shit the nun left in her heart—she left some words—I'm sending one dictation, they are all like that—words like chatter—crazy mystic nun—pobre Mary Rose. I care about her, Edw., and teaching, and children.

Pete moved into our house the day after we left—the kids live in the attic—that is crazy, a goddamn crazy thing how he won after all, without a compromise.

Love, Lucia

1961 [Spring]
277 Greenwich Street,
New York, New York

Dorns
Pocatello, Idaho

Dear Dorns and Finsteins,

Hey Finsteins, tell us how you're doing in the wild west. Rena, was it as glorious as we said?

Homesick for the ruddy blue sky. Raining raining here but foggy, ferry rides are wild and it is crazy at nite—shutters banging, fog horns, and after 1:30 A.M. the only other sounds are the horse-drawn fruit carts, creaking clopping splashing. Wow, like listening to Gogol.

Race has been on road last 2 weeks with Kai Winding (trombone), a good gig! He called yesterday, sounded so damned great, they have sessions every (all) day, are playing at nite everywhere from Toledo to Camp LeJeune and also good things like Detroit Jazz Festival. The band itself is sort of nervous and scary but he digs the way Jimmy Knepper (Max

& Rena—you met him at our house) plays (beautiful) and the chance to play himself. Also $ is welcome. He'll be gone till end of month. Yikes, we are lonely, esp. here in rain and all. M & J & I leave tomorrow for lake upstate with Race's Aunt Moe—which will be wonderful, boats and grass.

H, it is so good to hear from you. Tell me about Fred and Chani and Paul.

I don't have anything to say! I wash clothes all the time. Finsteins, Wow! Was it quiet and sad when you left? Maybe we'll use the rope and locks for our trip west.

Dorns, you remember that "El Tim" story? I rewrote it, wasn't any longer a "happy" ending or such a case study. No magazine (about 100) would take it, they said because it was touchy, the Catholic "issue"—the horny nun, I suppose, and last week a Catholic mag. bought it for 150 beans. This time no "creative" pangs or panic—I am knocked out etc.

Mark told me today that my eyes were full of red cracks.

Hope, Finsteins, you're finding a pad, etc. Damn, wish we were there. As it drizzles down hot water here, I think of New Mexico rain and clouds. Remember your (Dorn) trip to Alameda in the storm last year? (!)

Weird: the butchers downstairs sometimes work (very) late, come up the steps to the room where they shower. They wear heavy high black boots and speak German. Their sounds, at night, on stairs, very ugly. I remember the vicarious (baffled) terror from (childhood) war movies.

Made a swing in M & J's room. Lovely—the cat is wigging.

Love to every one of you. Lucia

October 24, 1961, 7:10 a.m.
New York, New York
(*Western Union Telegram*)

PROFESSOR EDWARD DORN
ENGLISH DEPT, IDAHO STATE COLLEGE
POCATELLO, IDAHO

LUCIA AND KIDS LEFT LAST NIGHT WITH BERLIN.
ABSOLUTELY NO WARNING OR SIGNS. SHE IS IRRA-
TIONAL. TRYING DESPERATELY TO LOCATE. GOING
TO ALBUQUERQUE CARE OF ERNIE JONES 415 SAN
LORENZO NW PHONE DI 46196.
RACE.

December 28, 1961
Edith Boulevard,
Albuquerque, New Mexico

Dorns
Barton Road
Pocatello, Idaho

Dear Dorns,

The mountains are covered with snow and it is clear and balmy, all the doors and windows open, Mark, Jeff, and the cats are on the roof of the shed shooting, like *Beau Geste*, the propped-up dead soldiers, the cats curled up.

Everything here is getting straightened out, and there is nothing anymore that seems insurmountable, though everything did a few weeks ago, Yi. No, I don't know Race at all either, it's very scary and not good actually how absolutely little I can understand what he or the Goodmans (for it gets indistinguishable who's talking) feel, especially since they keep, or kept (until we changed the phone), talking about Buddy and what a horrible desperate criminal fiend he is, consuming everyone, cruel and selfish . . . on and on. I don't know any kinder or cornier person than him. Yi, I didn't know, so many damn things about him and about myself, what living could be.

We're going camping for five days, tomorrow. Mary Ann got the Porsche and we got a camper, with beds stove refrigerator tent, it is crazy, the kids are flipping. We're going to Mexico, hope to get as far as Parral and see my uncle. If we don't hear from Race by then, will stay in Chihuahua and get a divorce (and some rum). God, it sounds so simple, is so simple. How little our lives were connected, Race's and mine.

Did I sound like I was complaining about Creeley? Can't remember, think I was surprised that he should be concerned at all about some of the petty aspects of our whole scene. No, he has been very great and we have had some good nights talking and laughing. Bobbie has been very depressed, with Christmas etc. Jesus, how cheap and stupid all the scenes are compared to that sorrow.

Like, Max, who was here, ate and slept here and borrowed a sum of money and rides and bus fare to Taos, put Buddy down, gossiped about everybody, and told me Rena didn't particularly care to see me. He and Creeley sat here drinking and Max was being catty and stupid, that's all he is, simply a stupid small catty man. Buddy and I left the room and we hope never to see Max again.

Creeley has to read in Seattle in February. He and Buddy were talking about the three of us flying to Seattle and then to Pocatello. There is a clinic there (Seattle) which claims to have a drug which will cure drug addiction for life. It's very damn hard for Buddy to stay clean, especially because there are so many people here determined not to let him. I couldn't tell you the nightmarish aspects of these sadistic bastards. Well, that will be OK soon, would be better with something like that drug, which Jean Lash could have gotten, but she's mad now, so won't, hippocratically. Yi, like, I was hip, saw *The Connection* with the original cast and read *Naked Lunch* and all, and said flip things like "it is like choosing to die," but I did not know. I shouldn't talk this way since Buddy's clean, but he is still not sure and neither am I and Mary Ann and the connections are positive he won't make it. One of them came on Christmas Eve (who fixes himself in his penis) with his 15 year old wife, his 14 year old daughter, and his dog, all addicts. Dog too. He is on parole for murder and it is impossible to let him know how I HATE him. I am terrified of him and what he would, could do, to Buddy, one way or the other. So anyway, we made it thru the visit, Buddy did miraculously, and finally they all left to go to midnight mass.

Otherwise Christmas was very beautiful here for us. We couldn't get up much spirit and carol sentiment or make cookies etc. but what was left was that here we were, all of us, on Christmas morning. The neighbors here are very great, came over for posole. Had a party a few nights before that was wonderful, with goodwill and everyone laughed and ate and had a ball. I had never given a party and Buddy hadn't either, it was too much, a celebration.

Buddy just called, we're going to go buy food for the trip. Got to go get dressed.

(Later) Pooh—can't go on trip after all. Imported Motors taxes etc. and have to go to Santa Fe for (more) of Mary Ann's signatures. Will be strange to go there without seeing you. Also, new mess with lawyers who are charging Buddy $3000 (EACH), $6000 total for the divorce. Very complicated, all these scenes and there are about 4 lawsuits too. He might be bankrupt soon. Max, Race, etc. put Buddy down for being a "successful businessman and not doing a thing." He can't do anything halfway—he's so involved with that overgrown scary business and it is too much really, how he manages all that.

Well, it was wonderful to see Fred and Paul and Chani—beautiful radiant Chani—how about that sparkle in her eyes! Fred, I would not have known at all, he is so grown and a young man, and Paul, that same shy sweet . . . Oh hell, I've looked at those crazy pictures a hundred times. I wish we could see you all. Write.

Love, Lucia

P.S. Hello. Hey, it is 1962. I never felt this way before, about a New Year.

At the end of 1961—the day I wrote above, Buddy and I went to the fuckirig lawyers to see abt the fee of $6000. The lawyer says "It is worth it, isn't it, for all this not to become known to police, loan companies, etc.?" (Mary Ann's addiction) etc. etc. Now like blackmail, only he is so self-righteous and nasty. So Buddy paid it.

We went camping after all for 4 days in the mountains above Taos—clear and beautiful (cold as hell), but the bus was warm and we had a ball, hiking and just sitting in the sun, magpies and crested jays. Spent 2 nights at Jay Walker's—at first thought he must be a big drag—like, he comes on about "making the sunset scene" etc., but he and his wife were great—happy etc. New Year's Eve we made the sunset scene and slept. Got up early, walked a mile in the snow on the mountain. Could hear music from the pueblo—very lovely and so blasted still.

Creeley just came over, said you sounded fine. Too much abt the job you didn't take, Edw.

Que más? We came back from trip so clear and things here seem so too. Will write soon.

Oh, and that connection got busted in El Paso. I'm sorry after all for him but it's a relief.

Love, Lucia

Dorns
Barton Road,
Pocatello, Idaho

Dear Helene and Ed,
    Yes, we are OK, NOT really groovy . . . can't seem to write
unless things are swinging or terrible . . . and things were so
terrible that it has been heaven to spend the past month just
being quiet, listening, relieved when all that happens is spring.
Grass came up at last. There is wind storm, four days now
and it's cold, 28 tonight, but if it doesn't do too much damage,
the yard will be beautiful in a few weeks. Coming from the
city was pleasure enough, just so much light and to go inside
and outside slamming doors. Have spent weeks digging and
planting . . . many vines and millions of those huge sunflowers,
and petunias that are even surviving the wind and blooming in
the middle of it, brilliant pinks and purples. The corn is a foot
high and the tomatoes all died, Cosmos are blowing around. So
frail. Everything else is about half inch out of the ground and
I hope, really, with all my heart they don't all freeze. It was so
crazy, how we planted them and they grew etc.
    Buddy and I were married April 26, Jeff's birthday, in
Bernalillo . . . Yi, it was like those people who have been married for twenty-five years and repeat the marriage ceremony.
JP was a Spanish guy, he improvised a crazy ceremony that
went "So . . . do you promise to love each others whether things
are good or bad, and do you promise to forget all of the past
and live the rest of your lives?" which was very damn lovely. A
raining spring day.
    Well, we will, altho things still seem like they will be so
hard, I wish it were two years from now already. Not so hard

for me, when I left in Oct. from New York, with Buddy, it was
because I wanted so much to be happy and to love, wanted so
much more. Just admitting that settled a lot of my troubles.
Buddy has been clean since March but that's still a problem.
More is the damn job and scene of just not wanting to do it
(Imported Motors etc.) . . . but he has been taking flying les-
sons every morning, digs this, and it should make the job and
trips to Midland and Odessa etc. more possible. This is such a
hard thing, the men I had known mostly or that I loved were
Paul and my father, and Ed, who loved their work or craft etc.,
or at least as with Race, this is what they wanted to do and
all they wanted to do. I think that Buddy had felt that marrying me would make a big difference, that caring for us would
be a reason for making the car-selling scene. And part of the
flipping in March was that it didn't after all make such a difference. I think it will though, we have both come through the
hysteria with, what, a lot more courage etc. If it doesn't make it
in Albuquerque, we will be able to split and seek our fortune.
I make things sound more gloomy than they are, or would be
normally (like, everybody's happy!), but we are both by now
asking so much of everything and ourselves and each other,
both had "gone along" for so long and can't make that.

Albuquerque doesn't help . . . lordy what a horrible place
it is, can never wait to get past the secondhand stores and furs
and get HOME, which is pretty great. In New York I never felt
alive unless I was completely alone walking around the city.

I have been depressed still about the loss of my writings
and my uncle's book, I really grieve as with a personal loss,
Jesus.

Mark and Jeff are swinging, tired and dusty, have some
good good friends, Tarzan yells across the mesa at six in the
morning. Here are some pictures, at Jeff's birthday party. He
grew up. Saw a neighbor about four doors down the road, said
Jeff had come to the door the other day, said "Hi, I thought I'd

come over and see what's going on . . . how are you?" They were fooling around in their room, moving furniture and sweeping, and I asked them what was going on, turned out they were fixing up an "area" for the baby. Both are really excited about it, feel it moving . . . Mark wants to name it "Mark-Jeff," Jeff wants to name it "Sharon-Michele." Please send suggestions.

Actually that's about the biggest problem going on, what to name it. I think it's a boy or two small girls, I am so huge and uncomfortable as I was in the last month with the other two. Latest plan here was that we help the Creeleys move to Vancouver and visit you. How about that? I think yes, things are really going to be good for them from now on . . . how fine it is to see how they are swinging together. But I'm not sure if I could make the trip, so might have to wait until Buddy has forty, or whatever, hours flying time. What will you do in summer? Oh, I would give anything to see all of you, it was wonderful to hear abt you from the Creeleys. Bobbie is great about drawing diagrams in the air and showing how big and expressions of faces. I feel I sort of saw you. She told me all abt the kids and the house etc., and although you sound it, it was good to hear them say too how great things are going. They are, aren't they? I think they must be, really.

My mother is in Seattle. Should be straighter since all she really wanted was to get away from my father and Chile, altho she is supposedly there because she is losing her teeth from malnutrition, which she got from the broken heart I gave her. I write her twice a week, for my sister's and my father's sake only, but no answer since October. Friend of mine in Chile wrote to ask how I was, she saw my mother and had asked her how I was. My mother said I was a whore and not her daughter anymore. Rhyme and all.

Wish we saw the Creeleys more. They don't come here very often and when we go there, the house is always full of people, mostly young admirers, which in a way is great, for them, and Bob too. Will be better in Vancouver I think, with more people to talk with.

Do you hear from the Goodmans? Well, I still feel resentful about their well-meant intrusion and possessiveness but I miss them both. Dennie's book was good and beautifully done I think, altho the Eichmann poems bug me, something very fashionable about them. Creelcy's book was really beautiful, well, the poems are beautiful poems.

Wish I knew more words.

Buddy just called. Yi, all this time I thought he was at the office, went flying this morning (he goes at six and then goes to work, before the winds start). Well, he was flying around all this time in a rainstorm near Las Vegas, landed in this blizzard of sand. Thank heavens I didn't know. He is really enjoying that plane, and especially early in the morning, says it is beautiful. Going to go at five from now on for the sun coming up, and I think he enjoyed the scene this morning since mostly he just flies around and lands, getting hours for a license. It is safer than a Porsche, though, with all these maniacs driving around. It is so strange to get used to cars. I do, actually do, miss the subways. And the ocean.

Did I tell you about going to Acoma Pueblo? Oh, I hope so, I have to stop, kids are starving for lunch and ate all the bananas. Do you need any chili?

Here's some petunias that blew off in case the color is still as lovely as it is now.

Well, we'll get up there somehow. Did you think about coming here, abt the kids staying here while you go east? Maybe timing will work out . . . do you, by the way, remember when first we knew each other and I had that efficient plan abt you going to Santa Fe in our car? Maybe Buddy could drive our bus up with Creelcy's things, bring back the kids, and you come later and . . . etc. Oh, anyway, I hope we will see you soon.

Love, Lucia

1962 [Summer]
Edith Boulevard,
Albuquerque, New Mexico
(*postcard*)

Dorns
Barton Road,
Pocatello, Idaho

Dear Dorns,
Looks like trip will have to be postponed. Baby could come any time and point is not to come too soon. So, we'll wait until fall and we'll all come and see you.

Have only seen those fat corn beads but haven't been to old town yet. I did get a bean pot on sale tho that should arrive soon. It had bugged me to think of that oven as it used to cost abt $10 a month to run it and you can cook a lot of things in the bean pot, or cash it in if you don't want it.

Well, phooey, had been so excited abt poss. of seeing you all. Have you heard from Creeleys? Send address if you have. Letter soon.

> Love, Lucia

September 23, 1962
Edith Boulevard,
Albuquerque, New Mexico

Dorns
Barton Road,
Pocatello, Idaho

Dear Dorns,
Hey, look who's here! Such a dear dear beautiful baby. Fat (8 1/2 lbs) wide awake and droll and dear.

Can't think of anything else to say, except we are so happy.
I'll write soon.

     Love, Lucia

David José Berlin
Sept. 20, 1962
at 3 HOURS OLD!

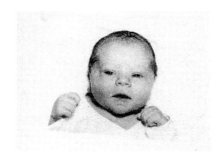

1962 [October]
Edith Boulevard,
Albuquerque, New Mexico

Dorns
Barton Road,
Pocatello, Idaho

Dear Dorns,

Next page is a letter begun about a month ago.

Since then my mother came (day we got back!) and that
was GREAT— Finally finally at peace with each other and it
was very beautiful—the whole scene (between us all, esp. her
and Buddy).

Then that next week came Buddy's father and mother and
sister—they're still here—his sister is lovely and it's pretty
nice, because everyone is happy. But a scene anyway, cooking
and eating and sightseeing. No no, we are swinging, or will
be when everybody leaves. David is fine, smiling and talking.
Good letter, soon.

I'm so sorry you worried, no need at all. Buddy is great—
and considering strain of all parents—feels great too. Oh, I'm
sorry you worried and I didn't write.

All love to you, Lucia

November 19, 1962
Edith Boulevard,
Albuquerque, New Mexico

Dorns
Barton Road,
Pocatello, Idaho

Dearest Dorns,

Hope you could make some sense out of that note . . . I'm
so sorry I didn't send a card or something . . . I started several
letters but never had more than half an hour to finish them
so I never did. Wrote one to you, Ed, about the Yugen piece.
Thanks for sending it to us, it was great. Yi, it seems there is
so much in it, I mean for a larger work. Great great everything you said about Burroughs. The whole thing from valid
premise or whatever (where Sorrentino's thing on Burroughs
wasn't, even though I agreed with him), as it had nothing to
do with the craft of the books. I'm afraid we've been hung up
talking about your piece with so many personal feelings, but
that's been good too. Anyway, we were glad you sent it and that
we read it. Have you more about the same? Seems it could be,
should be longer etc.

Buddy's family left yesterday. What a relief, but were actually sad saying goodbye, it had been very very good scene, with
everyone so happy. We ate (all the time) and laughed, they are
beautiful, so damned generous with their hearts. I love them.
They had a ball, mostly with the baby, but also they dug everything. We took them to San Felipe Pueblo, where Virginia

lives. She and Buddy's father became friends, he was very impressed by the way she predicted David's sex by my navel's position, and they argued over who had delivered more babies, and how (she makes a tea out of a black lizard when a delivery is difficult . . . he finally agreed that it would work). She asked us all to her house, they met the governor, saw real Indians drying corn etc., and were thrilled. Virginia and her family are so beautiful and quiet—you can't meet them and not get some of it from them.

With all the bad scenes last year the only thing that seemed to bother Buddy's father (who is sort of a drag actually) was that there weren't any matzoh balls in the soup, and most of the last visit was teaching me how to cook. So, this time I really put the pots on, like Mannie says. Kasha and Gedempte Flaish and tzimmes and stuffed cabbage and chicken soup with kneidlach, the whole scene (really delicious). Bagels flown in fresh from Brooklyn. Well, it was pretty nice, he was so happy to see Buddy fat and healthy, and with David. When he wasn't eating my fabulous kosher food, or kissing us all, he was teary-eyed holding David, saying, "Just imagine." Yi, I couldn't help but think of Race and Little Falls, that beautiful place, the trillium and lilies of the valley and the privacy of the people, excuse me for sounding corny, the aching solitude of them. At six thirty A.M. I would be nursing David and somehow everyone, Mark, Jeff, Buddy's parents, his sister, would all be sitting on the bed in bathrobes, everybody kissing everybody and wondering at David.

Yi, he is so lovely. Helene, I wish you could know him soon. He's gay and funny and relaxed and so pleased with everything. Laughs out loud, really laughs as if everything was so wonderful and funny.

My mother's visit was great too. In five minutes everything was straight. I mean really, for the first time in my entire life there was nothing but love and friendship between us. I can't tell you, maybe you know by now, how much it means to me to have that big sick load of bitterness GONE. I feel very different, like a grown-up etc., and so happy because there is so much now we have to say to each other. I must admit that when she has flipped with me, like that time in New York, it has been partly OK, her reasons, because she dug that I was not OK, that I was false and messed up. I was.

Anyway, it's quiet here now, cold and beautiful. I have to get dressed, it's 3 and time for Mark to get home. I've been fooling around all day sitting in the sun with David and folding diapers and drinking coffee.

Now that we can, we're hesitant about the plane trip to the north because of the weather. It gets pretty scary with ice on the wings and rain etc. in that teeny plane, so I don't know if we'll make it. I really long to see you all.

Did you hear from George? On Mark's birthday I called Fedway, to ask if they had a tent under ten dollars. This guy said, "Oh yes, Madame, we have a wonderful tent on sale, huge, big enough for two boys and little girls to play doctor in, just what you want, it's ten by four by twelve, etc. etc." He told me the wonders of this damn tent for half an hour, so I went downtown and of course it turned out that it was George who I talked to, and that they didn't have the tent after all! But it was crazy to talk to him, following him around this huge tent warehouse or stockroom while he climbed all over and under things, talking all the time. He's too much. Yi, there are so few people . . . at this point about the only bad thing (with us), there is no one who it would be really good to go over and see.

Mark's home, I've got to get dressed and comb my hair, etc. He is swinging at school, reads toothpaste tubes and traffic signs, everything. Is so damned delighted—has some real friends—is very very happy. Jeff is too, but he always was (and will be I think).

Anyway, don't worry anymore if you don't hear. Seems at

last things will just be going along here. I would have called you but there was always somebody here. But if you ever want to call, call 344-4141, person-to-person collect, so I'll know who's calling. I'll say no, but will call you back on the credit card for Imported Motors. I have no idea how it works but I'm sure Buddy doesn't pay for it.

Love to all of you, Lucia

1962 [December]
(*en route to Acapulco, Mexico*)

Dorns
Barton Road,
Pocatello, Idaho

Dear Dorns,

Flying over Sierra de los Huicholes! Crazy clear day—we'll be in Acapulco this evening.

Didn't have time to write, or to send Xmas package as I wanted, but, hey. I hope you're all well now and have a Merry Christmas.

Yi, we will—left Albuquerque behind us yesterday afternoon—flew through scary terrifying bad storm to Chihuahua. Buddy is a GREAT PILOT—too much to hear him call the towers—Takeoff is despegar, to unglue or unstick. I'm really with it now (the plane) not just that it's fun etc. but I've been navigating (abt the only way to know where you are by rivers and water-holes and lakes), so between the land and sky and the weather, you are part of the whole world. Right now over fantastic mountains, 10,000 ft., not a village or road for about 5 more inches on map. Just saw one.

Going to stay overnight in Acapulco, then fly to Zihuatanejo, but if you write the El Faro or La Quebrada, they'll find us.

Buddy just turned radio on, playing Mexican music! David is fast asleep on my lap. Mark and Jingo are bored by now and terrible.

1 P.M. Guadalajara!

Don't you hate it when people tell you what's going on while they're writing? I never believe it.

We're here—only one and a half hours to go! (We're ahead of schedule.) Whole trip, Albuquerque to Acapulco = 8 1/2 hours. It is BEAUTIFUL here. HOT, about 80°, palm trees and pink PRIMROSES, fuchsia, oleander, and RED gladiola. I love the sun, and being warm, and these people in Mexico.

Well, it is very damn wonderful to be here. We walked to the airport giddy and silly like last year (the first trip!).

Anyway, after storm yesterday and mountains (map said highest was 10,000, but we had to go 20,000), we barely made it.

We'll be in Pocatello soon. I wish you were all here.

Love and a Happy New Year, Lucia

July 15, 1964
Madison Street,
Albuquerque, New Mexico

Dorns
Barton Road,
Pocatello, Idaho

Dear Helene,

Your welcome letter just caught up with us a few days ago, via Oaxaca (bless those unpredictably efficient Mexican mails) and so did *Wild Dog*—with your very lovely cover. What a good issue. Wow, I feel so pleased to be printed in *Wild Dog*. Please thank Drew for me and Ed.

Well, we are back from Mexico, feeling very strange, foreign and homesick. It was a good (almost a year). Vallarta got to be too much. Alas, why are beautiful places, like Santa Fe, filled with people who can't stand anything that is not beautiful and easy (which is why we went there, I guess—it seemed such a sunny cheap solution).

We spent last 4 months in Chiapas and Oaxaca and Guatemala—mostly in house in hills above Oaxaca—very very great. Except for the damn fact that we had no "real" reason to be there and it is simply not our country (which is one reason for being HERE!). Anyway, you can't keep on sight-seeing.

The plan had been to build a house and to try to start some new scene—but got very discouraged about both those things. THWARTED AT EVERY TURN.

So, we're back where we started, except don't have the dream of "wouldn't it be great to just go off to Mexico." Buddy has the (really!) terrible problem of if he stays here and works at Important Motors he can make $20,000 a year plus the plane. But he simply can't stand it and if he doesn't do anything he still makes $5,000—he can't stand not doing anything—but if he has $5,000 there's no reason to do anything else etc. Bill Eastlake wants him to raise cows. Bill, by the way, had bad accident on his horse, pierced his lung and it really tore him up and shook him up. He's OK now but still very uncomfortable, and in pain. It was good to see him and Martha—they have many values.

Creeleys, we saw the 1st few days we were here—we stayed with them—a bad time to arrive as Bob had a lot of letters and articles to write. Bobbie was decorating the new rooms of their (crazy) new house and we were about as harried (?) getting back to Albuquerque as we were in Pocatello, when we were so anxious to get out of Albuquerque (I can't tell you how sorry I am that we were such a drag then). So we didn't see much of them and the kids watched TV from 7:30 A.M. to 9 P.M.

Oh, that is the saddest part. Mark and Jeff and David were so happy in Mexico, so swinging and simple for them. Like, it was weird to get back so soon to TV and popsickles and skateboards when only a week before they'd spent all day with Niko and his 60 goats in the mountains, in caves to get out of, in summer storms, eating bread and goat's milk and coming home every day with a dozen ADVENTURES and treasures, sunburnt and cut and scratched and HAPPY.

Jeff wasn't going to leave Oaxaca. "No, I'm staying," he insisted and later when he asked, "Well, will you ever be back here?" we thought he was sorry we were leaving and would miss us, so we said, "No, we may not be back"—thinking he'd decide to go with us—but he said, "Well then, I'll really stay." He keeps asking to go back.

Oh, I wrote a silly, what, parody of LeRoi's objections to people living in foreign countries—except that I agree with him (we Americans should be HERE)—so it didn't really work—except about those damn cheap servants (I'm so delighted to have a SINK and hot water and THRILL detergent and nobody hanging around all day). I always ended up cooking for all the maids and (their 10) children (so they did do the dishes). It is a terrible relationship for me, and we had only problems with David—big Freudian scenes with maids who were never going to marry because they would never have a child so beautiful and would rather dedicate their life to spoiling him more rotten. Dreams recounted every A.M. of they and David "alone in heaven." David, however, flourished. He is remarkably unspoiled—so affectionate and witty and silly and lovely. Sure of himself and loved. Doesn't speak English and on Double Stamp Day hollers from the cart "CALLATE LA BOCA!" to the whole Safeway.

We're in a weird teeny-weeny apartment somewhere in the middle of Albuquerque, near schools and shopping. M & J are in summer school, I'm shopping. (2 blocks from Levine's and fabrics and meats in cellophane, chicken peeled and cut up!) I could never adjust to seeing what the chickens ate. We're in a neighborhood which must be part of some sociological study or an Orwell book—everybody works—wives, secretaries, and most of the husbands at Sandia or the public service company or gas or telephone, married 2 years, no children, and for four blocks around it is DESERTED from 8 to 5. NOBODY. No hoses or cars and at 5 they all come home and shut the doors and windows and turn on the air conditioning and TV and sometimes a woman hangs up some laundry or a man takes out the garbage but mostly they do it on Sunday when they water the grass. (Glorious wet Sundays!)

I love the Sandia Mountains. And the LIGHT here.

The only other natural scenery that turns me on so much is fields that remind me of Idaho and Montana mountains—surprise clearings and openness—and is one sentimental reason I like so much the painting of Ray's. We sent for it yesterday—I hope it isn't too late. I'm so pleased!

Never did hear from Meg—and never did write anything she, they, might print either—except, almost a parody of her *Convention of Poets*, which was the accidental convention of (?) from California, metal men (welders, electricians, carpenters) we knew in Oaxaca. Crazy guys, 30–40 year old SURFERS who worked construction jobs in L.A. 60 stories above the ground. WILD stories. Made enough to spend most of the time surfing and turning on. Not "beatniks," whatever they are, but with tattoos and crew cuts and muscles and toothpicks. In Vallarta (we never saw them) to surf and fish, and in Oaxaca because they ran out of money up from Puerto Angel—were importing LSD and mescaline from England—legal in Mexico—to take to L.A., sell, and make a FORTUNE. Which, happily, they did.

They were the only Americans we met. Because we speak such good Spanish, I guess, and because we're sort of un-American, we had mostly Mexican friends. Which was sort of the gist of my unpolished argument with LeRoi's article. We didn't sit around with Americans as if we were in Cedar's

143

Bar (?) (I'm very out of fashion) or in San Francisco but did "penetrate to very innards of all walks of Mexican life." BUT IT DIDN'T COUNT. (Better that we should be so nationally culturally etc. strong—we should sit around in a sidewalk bar with, as Buddy's father would say, our own people.)

I'm still not sure why it doesn't count—but it doesn't. I'd rather penetrate into all these boring, predictable, apartments here (which I tried to do in that BAD "MAMA & DAD" Savage Nobleman story), altho everywhere we were in Mexico, all the people we knew had a BEAUTY (not sentimental on my part) and dignity (not false pride) that NOBODY has here. But it is FOREIGN to me—the dignity Americans do have has nothing to do with nationalism, family, tradition, religion etc.—it is truly personal and moral. Oh, I wound up feeling very patriotic and glad to be back!

I got very sidetracked. Please write a card—would love to hear about New York (Did you see Race?) and Buffalo.

Can imagine you all in your jazzy new convertible sailing over the Mississippi!!

Hey, when you get home and if you feel like it, I'd love to hear you, if we're here. Our phone is 255-9458. Please call, collect (we don't pay for it).

Love, Lucia

P.S. Please write—if only a card. I miss you all, very much.
P.P.S. I'm in love with Ringo and have a Beatle haircut (only just got rid of dyed hair).

October 15, 1964
1500 Fruit Street, NW,
Albuquerque, New Mexico

Dorns
Barton Road,
Pocatello, Idaho

Dearest Dorns,

I swore when I was a kid I would never say it . . . Oh, but Chan, how you have grown up! Thank you for your sweet letter.

I don't know how to describe how much better everything is, or why, we just got back from Boston and New York, but here we are and at about the tenth cup of coffee in the morning we lean on each other and laugh and laugh. Ai, in spite of everything (what, anyway?) everything's pretty great and simple. But, like, this morning we started dreaming of going back to Vallarta and Buddy said he'd fly down and find us a house and then come back and then we'd get a bus and all go down. The kids could go to school and we'd teach them at home. Oh, and maybe before we go we'll come up and see you. (Oh, jesus that would be so great.)

(David just woke up and captured the typewriter.)

Anyway, the fact that we're back right where we were a year ago (except I sold all the furniture and gave away the plants) has stopped being depressing, is in fact hilarious when you think about it. Buddy's father, 3 years ago, when we eloped, was talking about time, and life going on, and who knows what he meant to say but he said very prophetically, this is life, the world keeps going around and around.

Boston was too much, we wept most of the time we were there—like, Buddy's father, the spoiled querulous (old) bastard was too much, so damn sweet and sad and for the first time, so loving with Buddy—and the sisters still fighting all the time and worrying about which will inherit Uncle Dave's millions (we know, but they don't—will they ever be pissed off—he's left every cent to a 19 year old stewardess!). We went to see Uncle Louis in a horrible place for old people—like some surrealist hell—it was impossible to look into the eyes of these old men and women. We rode up in an elevator with a nurse and an old man in a wheelchair, paralyzed like a bruised skeleton and none of us, Buddy or Uncle Dave or I recognized that the old man was Uncle Louis, until finally Buddy did and he said "Uncle Louis" and the old man looked at him and smiled, with his eyes full of tears. Like, the nurse even cried, it was the first time in nine months that he had responded at all to anything.

Well, everything was weird and all the people like different angels or prophets from some Hasidic tale. Oh, and it was great to be away from the kids and to go to museums and hear music etc. The Boston and Peabody museums are fabulous. We had a ball in New York . . . Yi, it was so wonderful to be there with Buddy. Saw Henry, my dear bastard agent, and that was great, as was seeing the Kneppers. Except it turned out that because of that lawsuit thing with Mingus, Jimmy had a police record and did time in Lexington long ago. Mingus had tried to frame him by sending a package of bad stuff to him and simultaneously tipping off the FBI. It was so poorly done that nothing happened except the FBI guys came and asked them for pictures of me. It seems they think Buddy and I are smuggling etc. Which is OK because it is almost two years now since that crazy nightmare in Seattle and there is no reason to worry. The big drag tho is to find out that they listened to all our phone calls and still are and they knew of two letters I had written to the Kneppers. Whether they read them or not we couldn't figure out. Jimmy says it's me they seem interested in, and I guess it's because of my name in drugstores here and there (legal). Well, that and being followed and all the people in Albuquerque telling us they've been questioned, and the fact that Buddy never got bugged enough in Mexico to even want any cough syrup. All the other scenes here make Mexico seem very free. Plus the fact that he is so bugged he'd love a bottle or two but neither of us would dare to get any. I don't know how I got started on that, oh, except I'm paranoid enough to say don't write things about Tangiers busts and name people. When I heard they knew even about the letters, I thought of that and the like terrible irony of someone (him) getting busted because of my mail (like they know every intimate thing).

Probably the thing of New York that most straightened me out was not seeing Denise and Mitch . . . Jesus they were such a part of my life there, and after so many years of bitterness toward them I realized I love that damn Denise and Mitch and their weird son Nick. Yi, and I don't even hate my mother or Frankie Fernandez anymore . . . in fact nobody even bugs me, except maybe Bobbie Creeley and this little kid next door who is a dropout from the second grade.

Que más, oh, that it was so great to get home to the kids and New Mexico, even the jets start bumping around when they get around these mountains and clear skies.

(Oh hell, to get David away from the typewriter I traded for a box of Cheerios and the sugar bowl.)

Thanks for the beautiful Redon . . . wasn't it great to see them? There is one landscape in Boston with two figures . . . if you are there or near there. We tried to find Gene or Pat but couldn't, do you ever hear from them?

So long, I hope we see you soon.

Love, Lucia

Dorns
Barton Road,
Pocatello, Idaho

Dear Helene,

Hello! Buddy, Mark, and Jeff are off getting passport pictures. (I don't need one—isn't that Mexican?) So we're off again and very glad to be. Altho everything is in that moving mess—that's why I haven't answered your, or Paul's CRAZY letter (it made us cheery for days). Altho things seem better organized—we know now what you need there (EVERY-THING) and what to take (NOTHING). Buddy didn't get a house after all. The only one we're sure of is a little grass Arthur Godfrey shack overlooking the ocean. Which seems almost better than the little concrete box we were in last year and anyway "it's" all you need there unless you want to have a bubble bath or baked potato or something and you don't even need a house for that. So the only drag is that 18-hour, 180-mile jungle trip, from Tepic . . . parrots, flamingoes, rivers and MUD, and poinsettias and wrong turns. We four are going to fly from Mazatlan, and Buddy will get some friend to drive in with him, which will be great for us, and easier for Buddy (in a way) than with me and Jeff bawling every time we ford a river.

Hello! David and Jeff and I are waiting at airport in Mazatlan and Mark and Buddy are on that awful road. We just had our last Thanksgiving dinner (4th day). TOO much, on the beach under a palm tree—cranberry sauce and dressing and turkey, olives and celery even!

The trip so far was great—we're all in high spirits and happy—it's two weeks later than last year, and that much drier, so I hope the road in to Vallarta will be better. Mark is thrilled.

Did I say we were taking nothing—thought we had the minimum this time but that poor bus is bulging. We camped all the way down tho, but couldn't sleep, the sky was so starry and it was so quiet always.

Saw Bob the night before we left—hadn't seen him since his trip and it (England) sounded wonderful and so does he. Got the three writings of Don Allen—Olson biography was great and we really dug reading "The Camp" again, and by itself. Also sent the Coyote—thanks for all the information!

Gee—I can't think of anything—we've got 2 more hours to wait (2 gone) and that David and Jeff are getting sort of awful—so we'll have another Coke and David will spill it, then they'll have to pee etc. Then I'll have a beer, more Coke, pee.

He, Buddy, heard a terrible thing when he was in Vallarta from a woman from Tangier who knew Race. She said he got busted and was sent to prison there, for 5 years with no parole. Have you heard from him? If not, maybe you could write a card to Dr. Morris Newton, Box 613, Little Falls and ask where he is.

Well, I wish we thought we would see you soon. Please write and tell us how you are and what's happening.

All my love, Lucia

P.S. Thank you for *The Death Ship*. I'm sorry I forgot to tell you it came.

Dorns
Barton Road,
Pocatello, Idaho

Dearest Dorns,

Well, I'm very sorry I didn't write before to thank you for your care package of Ed's beautiful book, *The Peace News*, letter, card. Oh, if you knew how it cheered us both up—as did your card today—just when we are at a second low ebb (?) tide? Shit, like (we're very LOW). Moved back into Edith . . . Buddy got out of the hospital 2 days ago and is able to walk a little but is very sick and tired of pain—3 months now—the nerve in his leg so damaged it will be a long time before he's OK.

So, we moved back to US—it always seems so logical. Like, I can't have a baby in the jungle (altho it seems like a great idea now), Buddy's back, kids have to go to school, etc., etc., $. Oh, once we're here we can never remember why.

The house was abandoned. We still have to pay for it—nobody will buy it—we now see why—it is unlivable. The bastards ruined everything, the pool is irreparable, there is not one blade of grass, most of the bushes and trees are GONE, and most of walls. Everything is a wreck, plumbing, stove, walls.

I suppose it's philosophical and symbolic and all that—to come back to start ANEW—except there is so little reason—this horrid country, town etc., so repulsive and SCARY for us.

I went to Yelapa to bring back, and send back, our belongings—left Sunday and was back Wednesday. Had about adjusted to the idea of not going back there. Where there's no doctor if a kid breaks a leg, or whatever, and no school and no civilization. Was surprised on the boat trip—2 hours over from Puerto Vallarta—at how happy I was to be going home. It was awful to see the hills and mountains at the end of the dry season and I expected to find our garden a desert and was sort of glad—it would be easier to leave—but as the boat came into the bay I could see the bougainvillea and petunias from a mile away. A friend of Mark and Jeff's had come every day for 3 weeks to water (with buckets from the river)—he wouldn't take a penny for it—had just wanted it to be nice when we got home. The whole damn day of packing was the same—everybody came to ask about Buddy and the kids and to carry cartons across the river to the beach. It seems like ever since the bloody boat pulled out, and all those decent friends waving and crying on the most beautiful beach—I've been weeping. Los Angeles airport did me in—I missed Yelapa and our friends there so much I couldn't stand it. Very mixed up about our responsibility toward the children. In so many ways they are now like the kids there—how to keep that part here.

Had tons of bad and fabulous other scenes too in those few days there. Oh, Mexico! The last night there was sort of a nightmare which would take 40 pages to describe. Briefly, I got arrested and spent the night in jail, and the morning, until 20 minutes before the plane left and I bribed my way out. All started at Festival for the Sailors—where I went with some friends. I went to the bathroom, came out, and a sweet kid about 19 tried to kiss (etc.) me. 3 DRUNK cops appeared to arrest him (for rape) and most of all to go thru my purse, for $, I think, but I flipped because I had all these HEAVY bad things in it, so the boy and I tried to get the purse away. They started to beat him up and I INTERFERED and they took us both away. It all got very weird, apparently the new mayor wants convictions and they weren't going to let me go for 5 days unless I signed a rape charge— which I refused (all this went on in the Police Station—nobody else in town was around—

everybody was at the Festival). Then they wouldn't let me go until I "made it" with them and I got into horrible fight which brought my charges up to indecent behavior, resisting arrest, drunk and disorderly conduct, assault and battery (upon?) 3 policemen, vile and profane language, etc. The old guard threw me into the tank to protect me from the police! I was sort of Queen of the jail since I fought the cops and wouldn't sign any charges against "El Tiburón," my "attacker." It would have been (it was) nice, like the old guard gave me cigarettes all night and I cried and smoked all night with an 18-year-old kid in for 2 murders. In the morning I ended up spending 2 humiliating hours in the mayor's office. He could not understand why I would risk a scandal and not help the community convict these vicious attackers by sending "El Tiburón" to jail for 6 months or so, etc. I told him the only attackers had been the police and then he really got nasty, threatening, etc. Beautiful scene with "El Tiburón" (The Shark) who, when he finally woke up, couldn't believe I was still in there (having coffee and tortillas with a bunch of queer prisoners) and that I hadn't busted him.

Anyway, here we are, back at the ranch. Mark and Jeff go to summer school tomorrow and David to play school. It will be a great holiday not to see them all all day for a while, and will get them all adjusted.

Hmm. Well, it's wonderful you are going to England. Seems like the only civilization left. I wish there were Mexicans there and canoes and cormorants and pelicans. There must be pelicans? Thanks for turning us on to *Peace News*. Hey, there was an obituary in it for Olga Levertov, who I think is Denise's sister, a stripper who was very active in peace movements there.

It's Sunday and we're sitting around reading the paper—or Buddy is—I still can't get with it, or TV, or cars, altho telephones are a GAS—our number is 345-0852.

Don't have the plane anymore or we'd fly up there and see you all. I wish we could somehow, before you go.

Time to go for Sunday drive in the country.

We love you.

Lucia

A Note on Lucia Berlin

The Writing

Lucia Berlin (1936–2004; pronunciation: Lu-see-a) published seventy-six short stories during her lifetime. Most, but not all, were collected in three volumes from Black Sparrow Press: *Homesick* (1991), *So Long* (1993), and *Where I Live Now* (1999). These gathered from previous collections of 1980, 1984, and 1987, and presented newer work.

Publication commenced when she was twenty-four, in Saul Bellow's journal *The Noble Savage* and in *The New Strand*. Later stories appeared in *Atlantic Monthly*, *New American Writing*, and countless smaller magazines. *Homesick* won an American Book Award.

Berlin worked brilliantly but sporadically throughout the 1960s, 1970s, and most of the 1980s. By the late '80s, her four sons were grown and she had overcome a long-term problem with alcoholism (her accounts of its horrors, its drunk tanks and DTs and occasional hilarity, occupy a particular corner of her work). Thereafter she remained productive up to the time of her early death.

The Life

Berlin was born Lucia Brown in Alaska in 1936. Her father was in the mining industry and her earliest years were spent in the mining camps and towns of Idaho, Kentucky, and Montana.

In 1942, Berlin's father went off to the war, and her mother moved Lucia and her younger sister to El Paso, where their grandfather was a prominent, but besotted, dentist.

Soon after the war, Berlin's father moved the family to Santiago, Chile, and she embarked on what would become twenty-five years of a rather flamboyant existence. In Santiago, she attended cotillions and balls, had her first cigarette lit by Prince Aly Khan, finished school, and served as the default hostess for her father's society gatherings. Most evenings, her mother retired early with a bottle.

By the age of ten, Lucia had scoliosis, a painful spinal condition that became lifelong and often necessitated a steel brace.

In 1954 she enrolled at the University of New Mexico. By now fluent in Spanish, she studied with the novelist Ramón Sender. She soon married and had two sons. By the birth of the second, her sculptor husband was gone. Berlin completed her degree and, still in Albuquerque, met the poet Edward Dorn, a key figure in her life. She also met Dorn's teacher from Black Mountain College, the writer Robert Creeley, and two of his Harvard classmates, Race Newton and Buddy Berlin, both jazz musicians. And she began to write.

Newton, a pianist, married Berlin in 1958. (Her earliest stories appeared under the name Lucia Newton.) The next year, they and the children moved to a loft in New York. Race worked steadily and the couple became friends with their neighbors Denise Levertov and Mitchell Goodman, as well as other poets and artists including John Altoon, Diane di Prima, and Amiri Baraka (then LeRoi Jones).

In 1961, Berlin and her sons left Newton and New York, and traveled with their friend Buddy Berlin to Mexico, where he became her third husband. Buddy was charismatic and affluent, but he also proved to be an addict. During the years 1961–68, two more sons were born.

By 1968, the Berlins were divorced and Lucia was working on a master's degree at the University of New Mexico. She was employed as a substitute teacher. She never remarried.

The years 1971–94 were spent in Berkeley and Oakland, California. Berlin worked as a high school teacher, cleaning woman, switchboard operator, and physician's assistant, while writing, raising her four sons, drinking, and finally, prevailing over her alcoholism. She spent much of 1991 and 1992 in Mexico City, where her sister was dying of cancer. Her mother had died in 1986, a probable suicide.

In 1994, Edward Dorn brought Berlin to the University of Colorado, and she spent the next six years in Boulder as a visiting writer and, ultimately, associate professor. She became a remarkably popular and beloved teacher, and in just her second year, won the university's award for teaching excellence.

During the Boulder years she thrived in a close community that included Dorn and his wife, Jennifer, Anselm Hollo, and her old pal Bobbie Louise Hawkins. The poet Kenward Elmslie became, like myself, a fast friend.

Her health failing (the scoliosis had led to a punctured lung, and by the mid-1990s she was never without an oxygen tank), she retired in 2000 and the next year moved to Los Angeles to live with her son Dan. She fought a courageous battle against cancer, but died in 2004, in Marina del Rey.

Postscript

In 2015, eleven years after Lucia's death, *A Manual for Cleaning Women: Selected Stories* was published. It became a bestseller and was named one of *The New York Times Book*

Review's Ten Best Books of 2015. The Spanish edition, from Alfaguara, was named Book of the Year by *El País* (Madrid). Editions are out or in the works in thirty countries. New readers are discovering her work every day.

—*Stephen Emerson**

Connect online:
www.readlucia.com • www.facebook.com/readlucia
twitter.com/readluciaberlin • www.instagram.com/readlucia

*"A Note on Lucia Berlin" reprinted by permission from *A Manual for Cleaning Women*.

Acknowledgments

Thank you.

Especially to Barbara Adamson, Jennifer Dunbar Dorn, Katherine Fausset, and Emily Bell.

This book wouldn't exist without the publication of *A Manual for Cleaning Women*. Thank you to FSG.

Stephen Emerson, Barry Gifford, and Michael Wolfe, who spearheaded the effort to republish Lucia's work. Extra thanks and deep appreciation go to Stephen Emerson, whose extraordinary work and care made *A Manual for Cleaning Women* the great book that it is.

Lydia Davis, for writing the foreword to *A Manual for Cleaning Women*, the best we've ever read.

Jennifer Dunbar Dorn and Gayle Davies.

At Curtis Brown: Katherine Fausset, Holly Frederick, Sarah Gerton, Olivia D. Simkins, Madeline R. Tavis, and Stuart Waterman.

At FSG: Emily Bell, Flora Esterly, Amber Hoover, Jackson Howard, Devon Mazzone, Naoise McGee, and Stephen Weil.

Friends (old and new): Keith Abbott, Staci Amend, Karen Auvinen, Chansonette Buck, Fred Buck, Stephanie Buck, Tom Clark, Robert Creeley, Dave Cullen, Steve Dickison, Ed Dorn, Maya Dorn, Maria Fasce, Joan Frank, Ruth Franklin, Gloria Frym, Elizabeth Geoghegan, Lorna Gladstone, Sidney Goldfarb, Marvin Granlund, Bobbie Louise Hawkins, Anselm Hollo, Laird Hunt, Steve Katz, August Kleinzahler, Erika Krouse, Steven Lavoie, Chip Livingston, Kelly Luce, Jonathan Mack, Elizabeth McCracken, Peter Michelson, Dave Mulholland, Jim Nisbet, Ulrike Ostermeyer, Ron Padgett, Kellie Paluck, Mimi Pond, Joe Safdie, Jenny Shank, Lyndsy Spence, Ivan Suvanjieff, Oscar van Gelderen, David Yoo, and Paula Younger.

The publishers of the previous books: Michael Myers and Holbrook Teter (Zephyrus Image), Eileen and Bob Callahan (Turtle Island), Michael Wolfe (Tombouctou), Alastair Johnston (Poltroon), and John Martin and David Godine (Black Sparrow).

The family: Buddy, Mark, David, Dan, C. J., Nicolas, Truman, Cody, Molly, Monica, Andrea, Patricio, Jill, Jonathan, Josie, Pao, Nacé, Barbara, Paul, Race, Jill Magruder Gatwood, and Oliva Gatwood. Much love.

—Jeff Berlin